This book is dedicated to
Joy and Michael, Anna and Alex

Education as Dialogue

Its Prerequisites and Its Enemies

TASOS KAZEPIDES

McGill-Queen's University Press
Montreal & Kingston • London • Ithaca

ISBN 978-0-7735-3792-7 (cloth)
ISBN 978-0-7735-3806-1 (paper)

Legal deposit fourth quarter 2010
Bibliothèque nationale du Québec

Printed in Canada on acid-free paper that is 100% ancient forest free (100% post-consumer recycled), processed chlorine free

This book has been published with the help of a grant from the University Publications Committee of Simon Fraser University.

McGill-Queen's University Press acknowledges the support of the Canada Council for the Arts for our publishing program. We also acknowledge the financial support of the Government of Canada through the Canada Book Fund for our publishing activities.

Library and Archives Canada Cataloguing in Publication Data

Kazepides, Anastasios C.
Education as dialogue : its prerequisites and its enemies / Tasos Kazepides.

Includes bibliographical references and index.
ISBN 978-0-7735-3792-7 (bound). – ISBN 978-0-7735-3806-1 (pbk.)

1. Education – Philosophy. 2. Dialogue. I. Title.

LB14.7.K392 2011 370.1 C2010-904585-8

Typeset by Jay Tee Graphics Ltd. in 10/13 Sabon

EDUCATION AS DIALOGUE

Contents

Acknowledgments

I wish to thank my friends and colleagues Robin Barrow, Olga Costopoulos-Almon, Kieran Egan, Geoff Madoc-Jones, Suzan O'Neill, Slava Senyshyn, and Shelby Sheppard, who have read the whole manuscript and made many valuable suggestions. Grateful acknowledgement is also made for permission to draw on work published in the following journals and proceedings:

Journal of Philosophy of Education for: "Human Nature in its Educational Dimensions," vol. 13; "Educating, Socializing and Indoctrinating," vol. 16, no. 2; "On Educational Aims, Curriculum Objectives and the Preparation of Teachers," vol. 23, no. 1; "On the Prerequisites of Moral Education: A Wittgensteinean Perspective," vol. 25, no. 2.

Oxford Review of Education for: "On Learning from the Consequences of One's Actions," vol. 4, no. 1.

Canadian Journal of education for: "'Assembling Reminders for a Particular Purpose': The Nature and Function of Educational Theory," vol. 19, no. 4.

Proceedings of the Philosophy of Education Society for: "What Is the Paradox of Moral Education?" 1969; "On the Nature of Philosophical Questions and the Function of Philosophy in Education," 1970; "Wittgenstein and the Rationalists on Learning and Teaching," 1986; "Indoctrination, Doctrines and the Foundations of Rationality," 1987.

EDUCATION AS DIALOGUE

What is the use of studying philosophy if all that it does for you is to enable you to talk with some plausibility about some abstruse questions of logic, etc., and if it does not improve your thinking about the important questions of everyday life?

L. Wittgenstein in a letter to Norman Malcolm

Introduction

This book intends to serve as a contribution to the philosophy of education as well as an introduction to the discipline from a particular perspective; unlike other introductions it constitutes one extended argument that invites the reader to see education as dialogue and appreciate its intrinsic value. As I mention later in the book, there has never been an ideal society of education or dialogue, nor have there ever been perfect educational and dialogical institutions and appropriate social conditions in the history of humanity; we are only after an approximation of an ideal. The book identifies and examines the prerequisites and principles of education and dialogue as well as their main difficulties, rivals, and adversaries. My belief is that once we gain an in-depth understanding of the nature and importance of education and dialogue and identify their main obstacles we will be able to see the solutions to most other problems in education; we do not need superficial didactic textbooks with easy answers to serious philosophical questions. Like any other book in the philosophy of education this one inevitably reflects the experiences, character, training, values, and commitments of the writer and his vision of the good life.

The book consists of two parts. Part One examines some improperly used educational concepts by educational theorists, policymakers, and practitioners and brings them back to their ordinary everyday usage; its main purpose could be characterized as therapeutic and preparatory for the important discussion that follows in the second part of the book. As Wittgenstein observed in his *Philosophical Investigations* (#122), "A main source of our failure to understand is that we do not command a clear view of our use of words." Not only is the widespread and persistent talk about "the processes of education," "the aims of education," or "curriculum aims and objectives" vacuous, useless, and misleading but, as will be argued later, also shows the anti-dialogical and anti-educational character of all such confusing talk.

The first chapter examines and criticizes various claims about the nature of philosophical questions and concludes with the traditional view of philosophical wonder as having to do with our concepts, arguments, values, and assumptions; it aims at enabling students of education to speak about educational and social issues with greater clarity and depth of understanding. Philosophical thinking in education ought to avoid fashionable, vague, and half-baked ideas, high-sounding slogans, and sermonizing; instead it ought to use ordinary language and clear and coherent arguments and serve as a guide to our thinking about practical educational decisions and actions.

Chapter 2 clarifies the knowledge and value criteria of education and shows that in their absence we cannot decide what content is worthwhile, which methods and institutional arrangements are legitimate, and what kind of empirical research might be relevant or irrelevant to educational theory. It shows that, while the criteria of education are intersubjective, the content of educational programs should be pluralistic. The conceptual misunderstandings and confusions that surround "education" are not mere matters of language; they reflect our serious uncertainties and confusions about ourselves, our values, and the direction of our world. For instance, the omnipresent, seductive, and misleading talk about "the processes" of education, learning, understanding, etc. is the result of the dominance of the scientific paradigm in contemporary society and the pervasive but fallacious technocratic view of the human mind.

Equally careless and confusing is the incessant talk about "the aims of education," which I discuss in the third chapter. The ambiguous use of "education" by educationalists and policymakers is truly embarrassing and debilitating; even some of the most careful writers vacillate between "education" as "schooling" and "education" as an ideal of human development. Likewise, talk about "curriculum aims and objectives" is vacuous and useless; the assumed objectives, if they do not refer to specific content, are nothing more than uninterpreted, redundant, misleading, or suspicious slogans. It is my belief that unless we free ourselves of all this confusing talk about education and curriculum and their alleged aims and objectives we will not be able to engage in clear and constructive educational thinking and planning.

The second part of the book begins with the very important distinction between education and its prerequisites. Until now there has been no clear and satisfactory demarcation between education and its prerequisites. This section explores further the nature of dialogue, its principles, and prerequisites and the conditions that facilitate it as well as those that frustrate it. It examines in detail one of the most common and dangerous enemies of education and dialogue, which is religious indoctrination, and demonstrates the radical difference between doctrines and the prerequisites of education and dialogue. Finally, the book concludes with an original discussion of human nature that shows how human nature unfolds and develops under conditions of genuine dialogue.

The most important and original ideas of the book begin with chapter 4. As far as I know, no other philosopher of education has distinguished education from its prerequisites and defended that fundamental distinction clearly and adequately. The distinction is essential for educational theory, policy, and practice because it suggests different approaches and methods for establishing the prerequisites and different methods for teaching the traditional school subjects; as I explain in that chapter the prerequisites are *acquired* without the possibility of thinking, whereas all the forms of knowledge are *learned* and require the intellectual acts that are embedded in our various uses of language and the forms of knowledge and understanding.

The prerequisites of education are also the prerequisites of dialogue, although here the moral and intellectual virtues and the diverse "language-games," as Wittgenstein called them, take a more prominent place. It is surprising that, although the value of dialogue is recognized widely in our days, not enough attention has been paid to the nature, principles, difficulties, and appropriate conditions of dialogue, while the study of the crucial role of the prerequisites of dialogue has been neglected. The point of chapter 5 is to show the centrality of the prerequisites in dialogue and education. I conclude that nothing will improve our schools and our society more than rich and genuine dialogue.

After enumerating several intractable difficulties of dialogue in chapter 6, I concentrate on the serious problem of indoctrination, which undermines both education and dialogue. Once again the identification of the prerequisites of education and dialogue, which constitute the foundations of all rational discourse, will enable us to distinguish these prerequisites from doctrines, with which they have so often been confused by many philosophers of education. Some have argued that it is the non-rational methods used by the indoctrinators that constitute the criteria of indoctrination, whereas others maintain that it is their dubious intentions. I defend the view that although questionable methods and intentions are involved in indoctrination it is only doctrines that are both necessary and sufficient; the questionable methods and intentions are parasitic on doctrines.

Chapter 7 discusses first the obstacles to dialogue that are embedded in our character and in our social and political life and then concentrates on various religious doctrines that have been institutionalized in all societies and cultures. I trace briefly the development of the doctrines of Judaic and Christian theologies from old mythologies that have been made into literal historical events by the priesthood and show how all religious doctrines distort or undermine our moral code and form obstacles to a genuinely open society; all doctrines are arbitrary *stoppers* or barriers to our thinking that constrain or undermine our sense of wonder and open-mindedness on important issues. I distinguish between the literal and metaphorical interpretation of religious language and show how liberating and beneficial the latter could be.

The final chapter makes a sustained effort to connect our talk about education and dialogue with a discussion of human nature. The various claims that have been made about human nature are classified into four categories and an effort is made to see the relevance of each category to education. Just as education is not the natural unfolding of specific potentialities, human nature is not a natural given but a human attainment. Both education and human nature presuppose our common language and all the intellectual and moral virtues that are embedded in the various language games. I disagree with some forms of relativism and argue that there are indeed universal intellectual and moral virtues embedded in all the cultural achievements of humanity. Those excellences are at the foundation of education and human nature and must be protected from all beliefs, practices, and institutions that distort, undermine, or corrupt them.

Readers who are familiar with the work of Ludwig Wittgenstein will recognize how much I have profited from studying his later work and how relevant his work is for philosophy of education.

PART ONE

A Clarification of Relevant Educational Concepts

1

Philosophical Inquiry in Education

The limits of my language mean the limits of my world.
L. Wittgenstein, *Tractatus Logicophilosophicus*

Important educational problems are neither simple nor of the same category; they are both complex and heterogeneous problems requiring different approaches and methods for their solutions. Consider, for example, the general question that is one of the most important questions every civilized society must try to answer satisfactorily: "How shall we educate our children?" Sound educational planning requires that, in order to decide on worthwhile content, suitable methods and appropriate institutional or other arrangements for dealing with that question we need to get clear about the nature of education, its scope, and its importance; we must decide first what is going to be our destination, as it were, before we choose the appropriate and efficient means for reaching it. To do otherwise is wasteful and probably in some cases even detrimental to the young and to society. The same logic applies to more specific questions such as "What is the place of discipline and control within educational institutions?" Again, we must first get clear about these concepts and distinguish them from other related concepts, make certain that the forms of discipline or control we are considering do not violate our criteria of education and undermine the foundations of civilized society and then, and only then, consider their efficacy in bringing about the desired results. In other words, if we want to deal rationally with educational problems we must first address their philosophical dimensions, which have logical priority over any other kind of problems.

Unfortunately, the most common way many educational policymakers and administrators address these serious philosophical questions is by resorting to vague, high-sounding language and slogans that have, at best, only ceremonial value. "Education for survival," "meeting the needs of children or of society," "developing the children's potential" are some of the confused slogans that beg the very question they are supposed to answer.

What we notice is that teachers and educational planners are preoccupied primarily with the empirical questions they encounter in schools: how to teach a subject or evaluate teaching more effectively, how to maintain discipline in the classroom, how to reduce the number of students in each classroom, and the like. Important philosophical issues concerning the central purpose of educational institutions, the worthwhileness of what is being taught in schools, the importance of identifying and establishing the prerequisites of educational development, the methods that are used for controlling students' behaviour, the hierarchical organization of the schools, etc. remain to a large extent unexamined and without adequate justification. The extent to which educators today are successful in their task is due more to their reliance on their imagination, common sense, character, values, and commitments – not to their philosophical acumen.

WHAT IS THE NATURE OF A PHILOSOPHICAL PROBLEM?

As we shall see shortly, "What is philosophy?" is a philosophical question; in order to answer it we must do philosophy. Any other strategy will fail. For example, we can use a library in order to find out what kinds of problems a well-known philosopher like Aristotle discuses in his various writings. The problem is that Aristotle, like several other philosophers, has written books on a great variety of subjects. So we must know something about the nature of philosophical problems in order to pick out his relevant philosophical works. Well, suppose we simply go to the philosophy section of the library and consult those books that have the word *philosophy* in their title. Not a very safe strategy, I am afraid, because the word philosophy is often used in a loose sense, as in "my philosophy of life," where all that *philosophy* means is *my view or opinion about matters that have to do with human life* – this is a legitimate use of the word *philosophy* but not very useful in thinking about serious educational problems.

As we all have heard the names of some of the great philosophers, we are going to be prudent and pick out one or more of their books in order to find out how they define philosophical problems and what sort of problems they discuss. Although this strategy is definitely superior to the former it is not without problems. Philosophers often disagree among themselves or may offer woolly or unsatisfactory answers. How illuminating, for example, is Plato's claim that all philosophizing begins with wonder or astonishment? When Theaetetus expresses his wonder about certain perceptual and logical puzzles, Socrates tells him "this sense of wonder is the mark of the philosopher. Philosophy indeed has no other origin."[1] Aristotle expresses the same view in his *Metaphysics*: "It is through astonishment that men have reached ... the determining path of philosophizing."[2] The problem here is not whether philosophy begins in wonder but what is the nature of philosophical wonder that distinguishes it from other kinds of wonderment or wondering. It is reasonable to assume that wonder or perplexity is the beginning of all important thought, not only of philosophical inquiry; so the questions still remain: What is the nature of philosophical wonder, and in what ways does it differ from other kinds of wonder?

The first observation about philosophical wonder or perplexity is that it is not about the phenomena of the empirical world; philosophers are neither super scientists nor poor scientists, because they do not formulate hypotheses, devise experiments, and hope to discover some laws or regularities about the world. Philosophers do not ask their questions because some facts are missing, or some phenomena have not been observed adequately, or some experiments are inconclusive; as a matter of fact, they ask their questions even when all the phenomena have been observed and the facts gathered.

Philosophical questions are not about the external world we observe, describe, hypothesize about, and experiment with; they are about the concepts and arguments we use when we talk about ourselves and the world within which we live, they are reflective and self-critical questions. When natural scientists talk about certain phenomena in the world they use concepts such as *explanation*, *force*, *atoms*, *cause*, *effect*, and the like in their arguments, theories, and hypotheses. The task of the philosopher of science is to examine the concepts and theories that scientists use and the assumptions they make when they speak about the world – of course the scientist and the philosopher may often be the same person assuming two different perspectives. Likewise, we all use words such as *fair*, *moral*, *unjust*, and *caring*, when we talk about our fellow human beings and their decisions, actions, plans, goals, commitments, and the like. Moral philosophers examine those concepts and arguments that we all use when we look at ourselves and others from the moral point of view. As teachers or parents we talk about "learning," "teaching," "education," "discipline"; and as philosophers of education we examine the concepts and arguments that we use when we assume the philosophical point of view.

There are as many "philosophies of ..." as there are distinct human perspectives about important human activities and experiences. Thus, we talk about "philosophy of education," "philosophy of language," "political philosophy," "philosophy of mind," etc. Obviously, philosophers do not concern themselves with all our concepts or arguments but only with those that are central to our goals, beliefs, needs, ideals, problems, and decisions. Our purpose in philosophizing is to get a coherent and rationally defensible view of ourselves and, indirectly, of the world we inhabit.

We use concepts in order to formulate and express our thoughts, tastes, arguments, theories, and worldviews and in so doing we make all sorts of assumptions about the world and about human experience. The natural scientist assumes that there is an orderly external world; the moral critic assumes that people are to a large extent free and therefore responsible for their actions, and educators assume that children are capable of learning, that they are educable. All these assumptions and countless others have been and are still subjected to examination and re-examination by philosophers all the time.

Unlike scientific questions, which are about the world, philosophical questions are about the conceptual structures through which we understand the world. While scientific questions are primarily empirical first-order questions, philosophical questions are conceptual, second-order. They are derivative and secondary, arising out of the rest of our thinking about our moral, scientific, and practical concerns. As second-order questions they appeared later in the history of human development. But the secondary character of philosophical questions does not belittle them; on the contrary, their late appearance results from an advanced level of self-awareness and sophistication. An important corollary of the conceptual, second-order character of philosophical questions is that while the question "What is philosophy?" is a philosophical one internal to philosophy, the questions "What is history?" and "What is science?" are not internal to these activities because they are second-order philosophical questions; they are appropriately studied by the philosophies of history and science.

WHAT IS A CONCEPT?

It is one thing to say that philosophical questions are conceptual and another thing to get clear about the nature of concepts. Are concepts some kinds of entities to which our words refer? When we go to a food store we usually have a list of things we want to purchase. The words that we have on our list appear to refer to the items in the store. The word potato seems to refer to the potatoes in this bin, the word lettuce to the lettuce in the other bin, and so on. So, language seems to have a referential function. But is the meaning of the word potatoes those potatoes? If that were the case then what would be the meaning of the words I, you, here, there, now, then, and the like? There is no doubt that we use words to talk about the world, but the meaning of these words is not something out there in the world.

It has been said that the meanings of words are not entities in the world but the ideas that we have of those entities. Words, according to this view, are nothing but labels for the meanings or ideas that we have "in our minds." This view seems plausible and is held by many people. But is it correct? First of all we must realize that we are talking about "ideas" and "mind" in a metaphorical sense; the mind is not literally a container, and ideas are not like olives in the container. There is no use of the word *mind* in ordinary language that suggests it stands for an entity, let alone a container. We say that "she has a good mind" or that "she is strong-minded," that we are "like-minded" or "absent-minded"; we suggest that others should "mind their business" or that they should not "lose their minds" unless they want to "get a piece of our mind." It is interesting that modern Greeks will praise your creativity by saying that you have "a feminine mind." None of these uses of the word *mind* suggests that it is some kind of entity like a calculating machine, an instrument or a tool; the view that mind is some kind of thing is one more of those instances where, as Ludwig Wittgenstein put it, our language has gone on holiday.

If this view of mind were correct, then each person would form their own private ideas separately and we would have to explain how interpersonal communication among such individuals with such privately formed experiences could be possible. We would need a far-fetched metaphysical theory about mind and reality in order to provide a contrived explanation for such possibility. But this is not the only problem with this theory. If the theory were correct, then we should be able to identify "in our minds" our concepts, meanings, or ideas without the use of words. But is that a possible task? Can anybody identify "in one's mind" the meanings that correspond to the words "In the course of ..."? – I intentionally leave the phrase incomplete. What would such ideas be like or look like? "When I think in language," says Wittgenstein, "there aren't 'meanings' going through my mind in addition to the verbal expressions: the language is itself the vehicle of thought."[3] Language is not merely the exterior clothing of interior reflection that we may or may not use; it is intrinsically public, constitutive of our thinking, and inherent to our human nature. As Aristotle observed long ago, we are animals who have language (*logos*).

So, we cannot answer the questions "What is philosophy?" "What is education?" or "What is learning?" by looking behind these words for corresponding entities or ideas allegedly existing independently in our mind. Actually, the typical grammatical form ("What is X?") of traditional philosophical questions might be deceptive because it can give the misleading impression that they are about some kinds of entities that can be identified or about hidden ideas that can be inspected independently of language. Wittgenstein advised us wisely not to look for meanings but to look for the uses of words, symbols, and language in their everyday usage. The common mistake that philosophers make, according to Wittgenstein, "is that when language is looked at, what is looked at is a form of words and not the use made of the form of words."[4] We should be concentrating not merely on words but on the enormously complex conditions of their actual uses in ordinary language. "Every sign by itself is dead. What gives it life? – In use it is alive," says Wittgenstein.[5] And he adds: "Only in the stream of thought and life do words have meanings."[6] Our language, then, is not timeless, abstract, and otherworldly but expressive of real human needs, interest, and goals and is located only within human communities. (In the next chapter we shall see some of the serious confusions that are created by careless uses of *education*, which neglect its diverse contexts and uses.)

Words and their meanings are like coins and their values; there have never been coins that did not have value and we cannot talk about the value of coins that never existed. The distinction between words and their meaning is futile. Those who insist on distinguishing between "mere matters of words" and "the real world" are reminded by Wittgenstein that "we learn language and we learn the world together,"[7] or "you learned the concept 'pain' when you learned language."[8] It is only in language within a human form of life that the world is crystallized and made intelligible; to give up our linguistic hold upon the world is very close to abandoning it. When we fail to show sensitivity and respect for the complex and subtle uses of language we fail to make important distinctions and connections in the world and thus we end up impoverishing our minds.

Although philosophical questions are about language they are not like the questions of grammarians and lexicographers.

Philosophical questions are "deep disquietudes" that often arise through a misunderstanding of language; "their roots are as deep in us as the forms of our language and their significance is as great as the importance of our language."[9] Many philosophical problems arise either when we confuse the logical features of different linguistic expressions or when we impose upon language a preconceived idea of its proper function. In both cases, according to Wittgenstein, "we do not command a clear view of the use of words."[10] In a similar vein Gilbert Ryle maintains that "absurdities are the original goad to philosophical thinking."[11]

If philosophical questions are caused by absurdities, misunderstandings, or "lumps that our understanding has got by running its head against the limits of language,"[12] then the appropriate goal and method of philosophy would seem to be therapeutic – the removing of obstacles to understanding rather than the making of new discoveries. Although this is the professed view in Wittgenstein's *Philosophical Investigations*, it is hardly his only practice; there is a great deal more than therapy in that book. This self-reflective and critical nature of philosophizing has characterized the work of most philosophers, but it has been emphasized more in modern philosophy. As F. Waismann observed, while "previous philosophers have almost always directed their attention to the answers given to philosophical questions ... the new point of view ... ignores the answers and directs all its attention towards the questions."[13] And when philosophers direct their attention toward understanding the meaning of the questions rather than answering them they appear to be negative and destructive. This is true but with an important qualification; their operations are destructive but only, as Ryle remarks, in the way that threshing operations are destructive: they separate the meaningful and significant questions from the meaningless – not a trivial task.

Other contemporary philosophers, while agreeing that many philosophical problems are caused by conceptual confusions, have argued for and themselves practiced a more *systematic* examination of the uses of language. Ryle, for example, describes philosophy as "an exercise in systematic restatement" and the philosopher as a cartographer who rectifies the logical geography of the concepts we already have.[14] Likewise, J.L. Austin engaged in the systematic study of linguistic expressions and challenged the widely accepted view that the fundamental use of language is to describe. In *How to Do Things with Words*, for example, he distinguishes three aspects in any speech act: (a) the locutionary act, which is any act *of* saying something; (b) the illocutionary act, which is the act we perform *in* saying something; and (c) the perlocutionary act, which is the act we perform *by* saying something.[15]

While insisting that philosophical problems are problems of language, P.F. Strawson sees other even more challenging sides to philosophical activity. He argued that in order to understand fully our conceptual equipment it is not enough simply to correct conceptual confusions by describing how our ordinary language works. In addition, he says, "we want to know why it works as it does. To ask this is to ask how the nature of our thinking is rooted in our natures."[16] Or philosophers might want to view the world through a different conceptual apparatus and conduct their discourse about it differently. Strawson sees these two kinds of imaginative philosophical thinking (i.e., explanatory and inventive) as complementary to the therapeutic and systematic aspects of philosophy. Although many philosophers would argue that the inventive task does not appear to be very clearly defined or promising, the majority accepts the therapeutic, systematic, and explanatory tasks and perform them successfully. In this book we will employ these three approaches to educational questions.

WHY ORDINARY LANGUAGE?

One may wonder why so much emphasis is placed by contemporary philosophers on language and more specifically on ordinary language. Attention to the concepts of our ordinary language has characterized philosophy from the beginning; even a superficial acquaintance with the works of Plato and Aristotle would suffice to support that fact. To the extent that philosophers have attempted to legislate arbitrarily new meanings for ordinary concepts they have been unsuccessful and have been largely ignored by later philosophers. In education we have an additional reason to stay with ordinary language because the language of educational policy and practice is necessarily ordinary, not technical; those who depart from it end up using vague, pretentious, or high-sounding and misleading language and slogans.

Those who are tempted to use familiar words in unfamiliar ways should always ask themselves: "Is the word ever actually used in this way in the language-game which is its original home?"[17] If they ask that question, the answer will usually be negative and then they would have the difficult task of justifying their departure from ordinary use – something that natural scientists always do when they offer stipulative definitions. This difficult job of determining the use of the new concept has to be done always in the context of ordinary language with its complex patterns of connections and distinctions overlapping and criss-crossing. Ordinary language is not like a rigid calculus but is constituted of complex interrelated rules embedded and interwoven with the diverse non-linguistic activities of a human form of life. Wittgenstein compares language with an "ancient city"[18] whose centre is a maze of crooked streets while its technical scientific terms are more like the suburbs, with straight lines and orderly patterns.

Ryle argued that philosophers, unlike other professionals and specialists, should reject technical philosophical jargon for a very good reason: we know by what sorts of work and under what circumstances specialists (think of a chemist who has discovered a new chemical reaction in the laboratory) earn the right to stipulate new meanings for new or old words. What are the corresponding special sorts of circumstances and needs under which philosophers can justify their departure from ordinary language? Ryle asks: "What exercises and what predicaments have forced them to learn how to use and not to use these terms?" And he concludes: "Philosophers' arguments which turn on these terms are apt, sooner or later to start rotating idly."[19] To those who insist on questioning the thesis that we ought to proceed from and rely on ordinary language Wittgenstein replies in a similar fashion: "When I talk about language (words, sentences, etc.) I must speak the language of every day. Is this language somehow too coarse and material for what we want to say? Then how is another one to be constructed? – And how strange that we should be able to do anything at all with the one we have!"[20]

I know of no philosopher who maintains that ordinary language is the infallible court of appeal that cannot be questioned or corrected. Sometimes people disagree but, as J.L. Austin remarks, "a disagreement as to what we should say is not to be shied off, but to be pounced upon: for the explanation of it can hardly fail to be illuminating ... Certainly ordinary language has no claim to be the last word, if there is such a thing ... in principle it can everywhere be supplemented and improved upon and superseded. Only remember, it is the first word."[21] It would be prudent, therefore, before we succumb to any temptation to deviate from ordinary language, to take note of Austin's further admonition: "Our common stock of words embodies all the distinctions men have found worth drawing, and the connections they have found worth marking, in the lifetimes of many generations: these surely are likely to be more numerous, more sound, since they have stood up on to the long test of the survival of the fittest, and more subtle, at least in all ordinary and reasonably practical matters, than any that you or I are likely to think up in our arm-chairs of an afternoon – the most favored alternative method."[22] It is equally dangerous to think that our common language is permanent, unchanging, and infallible; there are all sorts of linguistic skeletons in dictionaries that are useless today, and there are traps that language sets for us if we are not always alert – in the course of this book we shall see several such examples. Our common language is dynamic and changing and can be understood only within the complex and constantly changing human activities within which new language games emerge and old ones are abandoned.

2

The Concept of Education

One must begin with the error and lead it to the truth. That is, one must uncover the source of error: otherwise, hearing the truth won't help us. It cannot penetrate, when something else is taking its place. To convince someone of the truth it is not enough to state it; but one must find the path from error to truth.

L. Wittgenstein in a letter to Norman Malcolm

One might think that *education* is a clear and unambiguous term in the English language; after all, it is not a technical term and we all know how to use it in our everyday conversations. We talk about well-educated persons, about educating the young, or about the educational value of books and experiences; but we also use the word education when we talk about schooling or the educational system of a country, about educational studies in a university, or about all the formative influences on people throughout their lives, as in the title *The Education of Henry Adams*.

It is unfortunate that *education* has all these uses, because if we don't make it clear in which one of its various senses we are using the term we may equivocate, i.e., we may use the word ambiguously, and the result is unnecessary confusion; readers or listeners do not know in which of the above senses they are supposed to understand the word. It should be made clear that the word *education* is not ambiguous, it is often *used* ambiguously;

the onus is always on writers or speakers to avoid ambiguity by specifying the sense in which they are using the word in different contexts. This may seem such an obvious point that readers may wonder whether it is even worth mentioning. And yet, many educational theorists and policymakers neglect to do this, which results in confused and misleading statements about this fundamental concept. There is an important difference between being able to use words in ordinary language and knowing how to describe the rules that govern their logical behaviour in different contexts and to distinguish them from other words. The first task requires common linguistic competence, whereas the second involves special philosophical acumen.

An even more serious set of problems is created by misleading talk about "the process of education," as if education were a natural process. This talk is a result of holding an unwarranted and deceptive pseudoscientific view of mind, which leads many educationalists to talk not only about "the process of education" but also about "the processes of teaching, learning, understanding and development." As we shall see soon, this kind of talk has created havoc in our understanding of education. If, on the other hand, "the process of education" refers to "schooling," as in the phrase, "processing students through the schools," then we have a different but equally serious problem. The consequences of this lack of clarity about education for the development of a coherent educational theory, the value and relevance of educational research, and the character and direction of educational practice are debilitating. It is apparent, then, that we first need to do some conceptual "therapy" before we examine the nature of education; heeding Wittgenstein's advice to uncover first the errors will reward us generously. Our problem is a complex and difficult one because the confusions about this most central concept reflect also our confusions and uncertainties and our conflicting visions of the good life. Following Wittgenstein's suggestion we shall start by clearing the ground from some of the most deceptive modern talk about education and "find the path from error to truth"; this strategy will enable us to see more clearly and correctly what education is all about.

CAN EDUCATION BE AN ACTIVITY OR A PROCESS?

The verb *to educate* may give the impression that education is some kind of activity, but a brief comparison with activity verbs shows that it is not. All activities have a beginning, take time, and have an end; educating doesn't. I started writing this chapter half an hour ago, but I didn't educate my students for two hours yesterday. Educating then is not an activity, although some activities may be educational, others miseducational and still others non-educational. Although claims that education is an activity are sometimes a mere infelicity with no serious conceptual consequences, more often they are misleading because such claims are about teaching or, more commonly, about educative teaching. Matters are more serious, however, with the claim that education is a process.

It is a much more important task to decide whether education can in any of its uses be described as a process. The use of the word *process* is widespread in educational writings. Perhaps there is no book in the field of education that does not talk about "the process of education," "the process of teaching," "the writing process," or "the learning process" and, even worse, about "the process of understanding" and "the process of critical thinking." Even one of the most profound educational thinkers of our times, R.S. Peters, entitled one of his earlier essays "What Is an Educational Process?"[1] But in which sense of the word *process* could we say that there exist educational, teaching, understanding, or learning processes? I believe that it will facilitate our discussion and enable us to evaluate the various claims about educational processes if we group the various uses of the word *process* in the appropriate categories.[2]

Legitimate Uses of the Word Process

In ordinary language we talk of a) natural processes (e.g., the process of digestion), b) technological processes (e.g., the process of manufacturing a car), and c) conventional processes (e.g., the due process of law). We do not use the active verb *to process* in the first of the above senses, but we do use it in the second (e.g., to process a certain material) and in the third sense (e.g., to process an application). We also use the idiomatic phrase *in process* to suggest that, in the last two senses, something is being made, constructed, or accomplished and that it takes time. What natural and technological processes have in common is that they are governed by causal relationships. Conventional processes, on the other hand, are determined by cultural rules that may vary from one society or period to another. While conventional processes are established in order to secure order, efficiency, humane treatment, etc., they may degenerate into unnecessary, cumbersome, and senseless bureaucracies. It is clear that in none of these senses can we say that education, in the important three senses mentioned above (educated, educating, educational), is a process.

Finally, there is another legitimate use of the word process, (d) as in the phrase "In the process of cleaning my room I found my lost book": this is an innocuous use of *process*, which we might label the durational sense. We say, for example, "In the process of teaching history I learned that ..." or "In the process of learning to fly I discovered something important about myself." In all such examples the phrase *in the process of* can be substituted by the word *while*. All that these locutions suggest is that human activities such as teaching the Pythagorean theorem and attainments such as learning or understanding the theory of evolution require time and effort. One doesn't become an educated person miraculously or instantly; that is part of the human condition. I mention this innocent use of *process* because, with a slight twist, it leads to slovenly uses of the word *process*.

Slovenly Uses of the Word Process

While not nonsensical, it is pretentiously academic to say that "in the process of educating the young we must do X and Y," but it is potentially dangerous talk if it leads us into the conceptual quagmire of "processes of education," "the process of learning," "the process of understanding," "the process of teaching," and the nebulous stages of educational development that imply such processes. All this talk, of course, may be just sloppy, careless, slipshod educational jargon. When in the title of his early essay, mentioned above, R.S. Peters asks "What Is an Educational Process?" he is in fact asking "What is an educational activity?" And those who talk about the processes of learning or educational development may mean nothing more than that in order for the young to acquire worthwhile learning and understanding they need time, effort, and a lot of care. In other words, the word *process* might be used in all these examples in its durational sense. And the stages of educational development may mean nothing more than that a lot of our important concepts and perspectives presuppose other concepts that must, logically, be taught and learned first. Unless, of course, they are not using *process* merely in that sense, and then we are dealing with pernicious uses of the word *process*.

Pernicious Uses of the Word Process

The belief that there is some order in the natural world is very much like the law of non-contradiction, presupposed by all our other beliefs and all our actions; it is what Wittgenstein called a riverbed proposition, i.e., a proposition that lies at the foundation of all our thinking – metaphorically speaking. The quest for the discovery of those laws, regularities, patterns, or tendencies that are constitutive of that order is as old as humanity. In the physical sciences the quest has been spectacularly successful, while in the "human sciences" it has resulted at best in confirming the obvious or the commonsensical – when it is not confusing or misleading. And yet, the temptation to explain human thought and action as if they were the same physical phenomena as photosynthesis seems irresistible to many students of human behaviour even today. Thus, psychologists and educationalists continue to talk about "thought processes," "processes of knowing or understanding," and "processes of learning" as if they were natural processes; but can there be such processes? Wittgenstein points out that here we have a "misleading parallel: psychology treats of processes in the psychical sphere, as does physics in the physical. Seeing, hearing, thinking, feeling, willing are not the subject of psychology in the same sense, as that in which the movements of bodies, the phenomena of electricity etc., are the subject of physics. You can see this from the fact that the physicist sees, hears, thinks over, and informs us of these phenomena, and the psychologist observes the external reactions (the behavior) of the subject."[3] Learning, knowing, and understanding do not refer to any kind of overt or hidden neurophysiological or any other kind of processes. "The grammar of the word 'knows' is evidently closely related to that of 'can,' 'is able to.' But also closely related to that of 'understand.' ('Mastery' of a technique.)"[4] Neither do these words refer to any kind of mental state. "Depression, excitement, pain are called mental states" but not knowledge and understanding.[5] I might be upset, depressed, excited or in pain for a while, but I cannot know, learn, or understand for five minutes.

Those terms that are central to educational engagement, such as knowing, learning, and understanding, do not suggest processes of any kind. They are all achievement words, implying that a person has come up to certain public standards, has mastered a skill, or is able to perform certain tasks. This is the reason our concept of education in its important uses that will be discussed below is a normative one; it encapsulates all the worthwhile virtues and standards of excellence that are embedded in the various disciplines of thought and action as we know them today. It is on the basis of these standards that we can decide whether an activity has educational value or the extent to which people, institutions, programs, or societies are educating or miseducating. Talk about "educational processes" of any kind is dangerously misleading because it draws our attention away from the "holy ground" of education, that is, the immense variety of worthwhile human forms of understanding, and focuses on the alleged processes of mind that are as imaginary as unicorns.

There are no natural processes of desirable human unfolding or development, although they are not unnatural either – even the greatest of educational romantics were unable to discern such processes. If such processes did exist, all our efforts to educate would be rendered unnecessary. There cannot be causally determined educational developmental processes invented by human beings the way there are such processes for manufacturing cars, washing machines, and the like; if such processes existed education would turn into a kind of naive social engineering and our educational institutions would become real factories! Like virtue, education is neither natural nor yet unnatural; it refers to an ideal of human development whose standards are social. The special character of educational theory, then, cannot be determined merely by the scientific study of human nature; it can be explicated only by philosophical inquiry and is inseparable from all our cultural achievements.

Finally, it is pointless to think of education as a conventional process. The fact that in the English language the word *education* is used to refer to both "schooling" and "education" is regrettable because this often results in a cross-eyed view of education: people who usually talk about education while keeping one eye on the schools. The majority of those who talk about educational theory have in fact been talking mainly or exclusively about learning, teaching, and schooling and the appropriate or efficient institutional processes that must prevail in schools. To the degree that this is happening, it is, in my view, a most unfortunate development for our society. Among other evils, it reinforces the belief that the other institutions in society can continue to be, as most of them are, to a large extent neglectful of their educational responsibilities. This is surely a development that must be resisted because it abandons the idea of the educating society where the whole community with all its institutions, laws, customs, political order, cultural achievements, media, etc. educates (or miseducates) its citizens. Pericles of ancient Athens knew that much, when he claimed that his city had educated all the Greeks; at our great peril we seem to have forgotten that important truth. The abandonment of the idea of an educating society is in my view one of the greatest dangers for civilized life. It is regretful that even our public schools and universities, which are supposed to function mainly as educational institutions, have become to some extent centres of mere professional training, socialization, or even indoctrination. What our society and all its institutions need today, in order to remain open and civilized, is a commitment to a clear, shared, and defensible view of education and, as I will argue later, genuine dialogue.

My belief is that the talk about the processes of education is the outcome of a pernicious form of scientism that has permeated our thinking and has contributed to the unfortunate institutionalization of the concept of education – education has become confused with the institution that is supposed to promote it and the conventional processes of schooling have become the processes of education. Thus, being educated has become synonymous with being "processed by our educational system"! The result is that those who have been talking about theories of education are in fact talking in most cases about the various functions of schooling. The confusion of "education" with the institution of schooling is as serious as would be the confusion of the concept of justice with a particular legal system. Without a clear and defensible concept of justice we cannot ask how just and well-founded a legal system is; without the relevant theology there cannot be any churches or temples; without a clear view of education we can no longer ask what the educational value of a system of schooling is. We know what would be the philosophical dimensions of an adequate theory of education or justice, but we don't know what might be the character of a "theory" that would deal with the multitude of diverse functions of schooling.

THE ORIGINS OF OUR CONCEPT OF EDUCATION

The search for a clear and coherent view of education does not imply any absolute views of knowledge or value; that doctrinaire attitude is actually one of the many obstacles for the development of a defensible view of education. We should distinguish therefore between the general criteria of education, if there are such, and their various interpretations within particular societies – the possible disagreements or variations among people should surely be informative and instructive. As with all our important concepts, *education* has had its own history and development: "what belongs to a language-game is a whole culture," says Wittgenstein.[6] As cultures evolve and become more sophisticated and refined so does their concept of education. We should examine, therefore, what kind of cultural achievements gave rise to our modern concept. One quick look at the OED will surprise us with some archaic uses of the word; in previous centuries people used to talk not only about the education of animals but even about the education of silkworms! In the Middle Ages, *education* deteriorated and became synonymous with *indoctrination*. Such linguistic skeletons belong in the proverbial dustbin of history and should not have any place in a serious discussion on *education* today. So we are not after an ageless, unchanging, absolute concept of education; we are after a clear, justified, and useful concept for our modern world. As we shall see shortly, our concept of education is contestable with regard to its content; it allows a rich, diverse, and pluralistic view of desirable educational goods and programs from which one can choose. No one can legitimately predetermine the content of education for all ages just as no one can predetermine culture; it is only closed illiberal societies that attempt to arrest culture and fossilize education, thereby impoverishing both. We must, however, have some minimal general criteria for the use of *education*; otherwise any talk about education becomes logically impossible – even if one is a radical relativist.

Our modern concept of education, as an ideal of human development, has had a very long and unstable history; its origins go all the way back to our intellectual forebears, the presocratic philosophers. These early Europeans, as they have been called, were the pioneers of an intellectual and moral tradition that has had profound respect for relevant evidence and rational argument. Heraclitus's plea, "Listen not to me, but to the rational argument [*logos*]"[7] is one of the earliest expressions of that revolutionary development – a radical departure from the previous traditions of sages, dogmatists, despots, and murky mystics.

This extraordinary tradition began with the abandonment of attempts to explain or control the world and human behaviour through mythology and magic; with the slow realization that our cognitive world is not a seamless whole; with the subsequent gradual differentiation among the various disciplines of thought and action – each with its unique concepts, logic, and tests for truth or criteria of success; and finally, with the discovery of the human mind as a unique and powerful organizing and creating force in the universe. Heraclitus no longer sees human behaviour as being caused by the whimsical gods of mythology but by the responsible individual agent. The god-directed individual of Homer gave way to the new, self-conscious person who began to examine and understand the world with their newly acquired equipment. It is no wonder that this new person discovers, with Heraclitus, that "a Man's character is his demon"[8] and not some deity outside themselves; or concludes, with Socrates, that the unexamined life is not worth living[9]; or declares, with Protagoras, that "man is the measure of all things"[10]; or breaks out, with Sophocles, into the most eloquent praise of humans: "Wonders are many, but none is more wondrous than Man ... who has learned the arts of speech, of wind-swift thought, and of living in neighbourliness."[11]

In Aeschylus's *Prometheus Bound* we have perhaps the most dramatic and triumphant culmination of human reason in this new radically anthropocentric view of the world and human experience. Prometheus's message is a dramatic version of Protagoras's maxim that human reason and experience should be the measure of all things – not the autocratic, arbitrary, and dictatorial gods of the past or the wishes, desires, and ambitions of tyrants, prophets, and despots.

The story of Prometheus, as portrayed in this play of Aeschylus, was a familiar one in the ancient Greek world: Prometheus the Titan rebelled against Zeus, stole fire (the symbol of reason in all its manifestations) from the gods, and gave it to humanity in order to free them from the domination of the arbitrary and dictatorial Zeus. But the autocratic and ruthless Zeus felt that Prometheus's action undermined his magisterial authority and should not go unpunished; thus he ordered that Prometheus be chained and nailed to the high craggy rocks at the end of the world so "that he may learn to endure and like the sovereignty of Zeus and quit his *man-loving disposition*."[12] When Prometheus is accused of betraying Zeus by "giving honor to the creatures of the day," he replies: "*I found them witless and gave them the use of their wits and made them masters of their mind ... all arts that mortals have come from Prometheus ... I am the enemy of all the gods ...*" The principled Prometheus will not compromise himself or bargain with the "savage" Zeus, the tyrant, whose arbitrary "justice (is) a thing he keeps by his own standard." Prometheus expects, however, that "that will of his shall melt to softness ... (and) he'll come ... to join *in amity and union* with me – one day he shall come." Here Aeschylus sets one important precondition for genuine human civilization: no whimsical gods or arbitrary authorities, no primitive power games or idiosyncratic codes of conduct, no masters and subjects, no exploitation of the weak by the powerful – but "amity and union" among all people. As we shall see shortly, this is a necessary condition for the development of genuine dialogue and education, for the growth of all important human virtues and for human flourishing.

Among similar myths in world mythology the legend of Prometheus is unique in its clarity, resonance, and significance with multiple levels of meaning, all of them celebrating human reason and humanity's freedom from arbitrary authority. In addition to its political message, which juxtaposes the arbitrary tyrant against the courageous rebel, it also contrasts primitive animal power with the demands of human reason. Prometheus emerges as the ultimate truly great philanthropist, the unequalled humanitarian and friend of human beings who selflessly suffers for our sake; with his "man-loving disposition," as Aeschylus describes him, he appears to be just like us, or rather the best in us. He is our great liberator and benefactor; now we are challenged to determine our lives with knowledge and understanding alone – the wishes, needs, and desires of the gods and other tyrants are irrelevant to our lives.

Our concept of education emerged and developed out of such momentous intellectual and moral changes of outlook and refers to the unique formative powers of our own human achievements (in art and literature, philosophy, science, morality, and the other forms of human excellences) for the development of the human mind as well as for the character and proper direction of our civilization. Before these discoveries and outlooks, or outside such discoveries, there cannot be any talk about education. That is why we cannot regard even a Homeric hero such as the cunning Odysseus or the "wise man" of a primitive tribe as educated. To be educated is not merely to have acquired certain skills, habits, beliefs, attitudes, and values that are deemed desirable or useful by the particular social group to which a person belongs – that is what sociologists call socialization; it is rather to have one's mind and character disciplined by the logic and the standards of excellence immanent in the various disciplines of thought and action and their respective norms and language games as we practice them today. The aim of educational institutions then should not be the mere furnishing of the mind with what Whitehead called "inert ideas" – "the learning of many things," said Heraclitus long before him, "does not develop one's mind"[13] – but the development of the ability to recognize the demands of reason in its various forms and to fulfill them. It is obvious that this aim can be achieved only through an introduction into the established content and methodology of the various forms of human awareness and understanding. As the young acquire knowledge they learn what it means to pursue truth – rather than approval, security, comfort, or peace of mind – and why truth matters supremely for humanity; they also learn why the pursuit of truth is inseparable from the principles of respect for evidence and sound argument, freedom of thought, consistency, clarity, and all the other moral and intellectual principles.

These are not persuasive or programmatic claims seeking to alter the meaning of *education* for some hidden purposes; in its central and most important uses *education* is inseparable from all human excellences and the demands of reason that are embedded in them. We should be very perplexed, as would Heraclitus, by the remark: "Here is an educated person who has no worthwhile knowledge or understanding whatsoever." There is, of course, that other sense of *education*, which is synonymous with all learning or socialization (as, for example, in the phrase, "The education of Henry Adams"). It is hard to see, however, how this broad sense of education could be of any use to educators looking for signposts to give direction to their thinking and decision-making on serious educational matters. We will postpone for later the discussion of education as socialization.

THE CRITERIA OF EDUCATION

As indicated earlier, it might be misleading to talk about "the concept of education" because it may give the impression that *education* refers exclusively to the institution of schooling or, worse, to some kind of a private idea in our minds that we are expected to identify or locate. As always, it is advisable to look at the various uses of *education* in ordinary language.

The three important uses of the word are to be found in the participial adjective (*the educated*), the verb (*to educate*), and the adjective (*educational*). In ordinary language we ask whether somebody is an educated person, whether teachers are educating their students, or whether an activity or program has educational value.

What these three uses have in common is that they imply a certain ideal of human development,[14] worthwhile content, and appropriate educational methods; the concept of education that is involved in these uses is normative, governed by criteria of knowledge and worthwhileness and their immanent intellectual and moral virtues, which we will discuss later. We cannot say that a person is educated but has no knowledge and understanding or that their knowledge is worthless; none of the other descriptive uses of *education* mentioned earlier and none of the other terms that are related to education (such as learning or teaching, rearing, or upbringing) requires worthwhile knowledge determined by intersubjective criteria. It is a conceptual truth that the contemporary use of *education* in its normative sense implies knowledge and understanding that we consider worthwhile, although its specific content cannot be established by appealing only to the rules that govern the concept of education – for that we need different kinds of arguments. A person who does not accept knowledge and worthwhileness as criteria of education but persists in using the word is simply thinking and talking about something else, for example, upbringing, socialization, indoctrination, teaching, training, and the like.

The Knowledge Criterion

The knowledge criterion is central to education because it enables us to distinguish among justified beliefs and arbitrary doctrines, unfounded beliefs, personal biases, fantasies, opinions, prejudices, or mere preferences. Unlike the latter, knowledge claims always require appropriate evidence or reasons that are intersubjective; if one person claims knowing X on the basis of relevant evidence or reasons, every other person, in principle, should be also entitled to make the same knowledge claim. Private knowledge that cannot be communicated to others and appropriately supported is impossible, and those who claim to have such knowledge are usually quacks, charlatans, indoctrinators, or simpletons – unless, of course, they are speaking metaphorically; we will discuss the metaphorical uses of language later when we discuss indoctrination.

That the world exists is a deep, unfathomable, and irresolvable mystery; no one knows why the world exists, and that is the reason some people resort to metaphor or mythology – the only permissible ways to talk about this yawning mystery. But we can discover *how* the world is if we work patiently, carefully, and systematically, the way scientists do, and avoid arbitrary claims. It is only through knowledge that we can gain some genuine understanding of ourselves and the world we inhabit – not through doctrines, prejudices, and the like. There is an unbridgeable intellectual abyss between the person who believes the biblical myth of creation literally and the person who has studied science and the theory of evolution. For the truly educated person any arbitrary, careless, hasty, and frivolous claims made about the world are cases of human hubris or, as Bertrand Russell called them, forms of "cosmic impiety"; the proper attitude toward the world for any thoughtful, temperate, disciplined, and prudent person is one of awe, wonder, marvel, and astonishment.

As we shall see later, knowledge and the intellectual and moral virtues that sustain it are prerequisites for all genuine dialogue and human flourishing. Among the virtues that are inseparable for the pursuit of knowledge, such as clarity, consistency, coherence, respect for evidence and cogent arguments, freedom of thought, impartiality, etc., we must mention here commitment to truth as fundamental to all our rational thinking and acting. It is presupposed by every one of the countless ordinary uses of language (hereafter, language games) such as asking questions, describing things, reporting events, explaining or predicting phenomena, evaluating arguments or proposals, expressing our opinions, promising, confessing, or criticizing. Truth matters supremely because it would be unthinkable to imagine any language game or even any human society without that concept; any violation of this or other principles can be understood only as betrayal of reason or as falling short of the demands of reason. And that is why I find Richard Rorty's comment that we should think of "'true' as a word which applies to those beliefs upon which we are able to agree" and that it is "entirely a matter of solidarity"[15] to be not only mistaken but frivolous and distasteful. "We" might be religious fundamentalists, racists or sexists, slave-owners or members of Stalin's or Hitler's circles of thugs, or the Taliban. Words have their paradigmatic contexts and talk about "solidarity" might be a desirable slogan in the political world, depending entirely on the principles that lead to solidarity; we would wish rather that all the evil, ignorant, or mad people lack or had lacked solidarity. It is a puzzle for me how a chameleonic political slogan about "solidarity" could function as an appropriate criterion of what is true!

But the educated person is not merely knowledgeable, nor a dilettante who has superficial knowledge on many subjects and manages to impress people at cocktail parties; to mention Heraclitus's point again: "The learning of many things does not develop one's mind." Education is about the development of the mind and character of persons, not merely about furnishing their minds with information or "'inert ideas' – that is to say, ideas that are merely received into the mind without being utilized, or tested, or thrown into fresh combinations."[16] Ideally educated persons are able to pursue any subject in some depth describing phenomena with clarity and precision, explaining why certain things are the case, talking about works of art, music, and literature in an informed way, evaluating arguments with appropriate criteria and knowledge, examining their own beliefs, assumptions, commitments, and the like. They are not passive recipients of ideas; they are active thinkers, and they are able to distinguish between those things that are required by reason and those that are allowed by reason; they can see what is literally true or false and what might be metaphorically appropriate or unsuitable in specific circumstances. "To be educated," said R.S. Peters very aptly, "is not to have arrived at a destination; it is to travel with a different view"; it involves the understanding of underlying principles and a broad cognitive perspective.[17] Those who "have completed their education," i.e., their schooling, will continue their education after graduation, if their schooling has been successful in putting them on their way to self-education; education does not have an end and one can never graduate from education. One may find John Dewey's view of education too demanding or exhausting, but at its best "education is the constant reorganizing and reconstructing of experience."[18] It is because educated persons are transformed persons, or rather persons in continuous transformation, that we expect them to talk, think, feel, and act differently, i.e., according to the demands of reason that are enshrined in various forms of knowledge, language games, and activities. "Culture," said Alfred North Whitehead (and he was talking about education), "is activity of thought, and receptiveness to beauty and humane feeling. Scraps of information have nothing to do with it."[19]

Educated persons differ from trained persons in that they have an understanding of fundamental principles and some breadth of knowledge and understanding. We talk of people being trained *in* auto mechanics, *as* soldiers, or *for* a specific job, but we do not talk of people being educated *in*, *as*, or *for* anything. Peters makes that point very succinctly when he asks us to consider what is involved in sex education as opposed to sex training! The educated person's mind is not merely trained or informed but transformed by the various forms of knowledge and understanding in which it is actively engaged. In our day we expect educated people to have acquired sufficient understanding of the various forms of human inquiry such as science, morality, art and music, philosophy, and history, so that they can have an informed perspective on themselves and the world. The educated person must have both some breadth and some depth of knowledge and understanding. But, just as we should be wary of people who have read only one book, we should also be concerned about people who have read many superficial books.

The knowledge criterion enables us not only to choose the appropriate content of education but also the methods and institutional arrangements appropriate to the task of educating the young. Methods and procedures such as conditioning, which bypass the student's mind, cannot be used by educators to impart knowledge and thus develop the mind. Learners must not only be aware of what is happening to them but must also be actively and critically engaged in learning and using their knowledge. Later we will make a key distinction between *learning*, which is appropriate to the educational engagement, and *acquisition*, which is suitable for establishing the prerequisites of education.

Being educated is a matter of degree, and we cannot decide in general where we should draw the line between the educated and the uneducated; like other important concepts, *education* is vague. We know that Leonardo da Vinci was a superbly educated person, and we do not have any doubts that a newly born baby is a paradigm case of an uneducated human being. We are not always certain, however, about the degree to which an average high school graduate is an educated person; it depends on our expectations, the knowledge that is available, the standards and social conditions that are prevalent in a particular society, the degree to which the graduate has been transformed, and so on. "The educated person" is not an objective that can be reached but an ideal that can be only striven toward.

The Value Criterion

According to Aristotle, "All human beings desire to know by nature."[20] The quest for knowledge is natural to all humans, sometimes for its own sake and sometimes for its instrumental value. We can see that desire for knowledge in the way even very young children explore their environment and in their constant questioning about things, events, or reasons. In complex societies like our own the organized transmission of worthwhile knowledge has become a social necessity; the acquisition of knowledge in some depth and breadth by the young is of great value for the wellbeing both of the young and of society. Our whole civilization today is based on knowledge and understanding and our schools are supposed to teach those subjects that are required for worthwhile living and for dealing with our complex world.

All human activities are pursued either for their intrinsic or instrumental value, but usually for both. I can think of some activities, such as visiting the dentist, taking out the garbage, or vacuuming the house, that I perform purely for their instrumental value; they are not goods in and of themselves. On the other hand, I may chose to take the subway rather than drive because I enjoy riding the subway and I also want to spend the time reading that fascinating book that I started yesterday – now I have chosen an instrumental-intrinsic good in order to enjoy another intrinsic good. The justification of actions we perform for their instrumental value lies in their efficiency in securing another end, instrumental or intrinsic. But instrumental thinking and acting must sooner or later come to an end; we would be slaves trapped in a vicious cycle if we did not have a chance in the end to pursue some activities for their own sake, for what is in them that we prize. One might even claim that the best society is the one that manages to require of its citizens the fewest instrumental activities while providing the greatest number of intrinsic goods.

Intrinsic goods are desirable for their own sake; we enjoy eating, having sex, reading a good book, appreciating a great work of art or music, talking to a good friend, being able to help others, doing science or philosophy, and countless other activities. We cannot establish a hierarchy among intrinsic goods and cannot compare them; each one of them provides us with a special satisfaction or a special perspective on ourselves and the world. What is special about the forms of knowledge I mentioned earlier is that they equip us with unique perspectives and should, therefore, be part of the educational diet of every citizen. Their intrinsic value lies in the fact that they are indispensable for the development, cultivation, and growth of the human mind and that is the reason they are deemed to be "the holy ground" of education: without them the human mind cannot develop in its varied, important, subtle, and sophisticated ways. One would expect, then, that all the forms of understanding would be taught in our schools, but they rarely are. I don't know many public schools that teach philosophy as one of their subjects, and music and art are often among the most neglected subjects. In our consumer-oriented utilitarian society, where instrumental reasoning has become dominant, the intrinsic value of these areas of study is not apparent to the politicians, lawmakers, and generals. Every time decision-makers are faced with another problem in the unrelenting struggle for economic growth or domination they call for more math and science in the schools on the assumption that these subjects have greater utilitarian value for our technological world. What drives educational planning worldwide today is not a vision of the good, just, and peaceful society but the economy and its handmaid, technology – as if these were panaceas for all social problems.

Of course, every good teacher and all educated people know that it is important for students to appreciate the intrinsic value of a subject – any subject. The instrumental value of their knowledge would be even greater if both teachers and learners pursued their subjects for their own sake, for what is in them rather than for what they can lead to. Here, then, is one important criterion of good teaching: can a teacher appreciate and delight in the intrinsic value of a given subject and convey that delight, care, commitment and sense of wonder to students? With the exception of some monotonous activities, like the ones I mentioned earlier, the overwhelming majority of human activities can be pursued for their intrinsic interest by most people. The forms of knowledge and all other worthwhile activities are among those that can arouse a deep sense of wonder in the educated teacher, which, in turn, can awaken students' curiosity and desire to study them more thoroughly, systematically, and in depth. This is when teaching becomes truly dialogic and involves teacher and learners in a common exploration where the teacher's provisional authority surrenders to the epistemic standards and demands of the subject under investigation and to respect for students as equals before the common task. If educative teaching is about developing worthwhile interests in the young, I cannot think of a better way to accomplish that goal. When teaching becomes dialogic it moves away from mere telling, giving orders, haranguing, sermonizing, lecturing, and even training – all of which tend to reinforce the passivity of the learners – and makes the students active and dynamic participants in their learning.

There are countless human activities that we can pursue for their intrinsic value, but we are not born endowed by nature to develop and pursue all of them regardless of the circumstances of our lives; they are social human achievements and must be learned under appropriate circumstances. The forms of knowledge have a privileged position in any educational curriculum because they provide us with the most sophisticated understanding of ourselves and the world we inhabit; their intrinsic value becomes obvious and motivates us as we understand their character, the light they shed on human experience, and the unique perspective each one of them enables us to develop. We do not know which form or forms of understanding young people will decide to pursue in depth later in their lives; that depends on many factors. What we owe our young is the opportunity to get to know as many of the forms in some depth so that they can appreciate their unique value and pursue them for that reason rather than merely for their instrumental value; it is in the long-term interest and happiness of the young that they pursue worthwhile activities for what is in them.

A person who has been initiated into the various forms of understanding may choose to pursue some of them in some depth and then abandon them in order to explore other forms more fully. It is exceptional to find a person who pursues science and philosophy, history and art, music and mathematics simultaneously with the same passion – there are not many Leonardos in the world. As well, there are other worthwhile things in life outside the pursuit of the forms of knowledge. So one can pursue science for a while and then decide to take a long vacation and travel around the world or pick up painting or music without bothering to keep up with the latest developments in one's former discipline. The only tenable position with regard to the specific *content* of the forms of understanding is a pluralistic one; as long as a person has been initiated into each form and understands its basic concepts, principles, and methodology and the unique perspective it provides, one can have a wide choice of activities to choose from; unless of course the educator is a Procrustean who wants people to conform to his personal preferences or an indoctrinator who desires to arrest or limit intellectual development.

Commitment to the Demands of Reason

Educated persons may pursue any of a number of worthwhile activities in some depth and breadth; they may want to learn more history, science, philosophy, music, or art; they must be able to recognize the essential demands of reason in each one of the forms of knowledge and understanding. The highest point in all learning is neither learning that something is the case nor learning to do something but learning to be a certain kind of person, i.e., a person who not only recognizes the demands of reason but also becomes committed to them and is transformed by them. We don't expect educated people to be omniscient or infallible; we don't refuse to call a person educated because they are uninformed about the Middle Ages or the theory of relativity, but no one can claim to be educated if they do not care about truth, adequate evidence for their beliefs, consistency and clarity in their thinking, fairness and respect for other people, etc. Unlike specific content, these principles are not matters of choice or preference for the educated person; they are part of what it means to be educated and no one should be indifferent to them. We shall revisit the importance of the demands of reason for education later when we talk about dialogue and human nature. But it is worth mentioning that the source of most of our social problems today is not the lack of specific knowledge about the latest developments in engineering, medicine, physics, mathematics, astronomy, or any other subject; it is that too many people have failed to commit themselves to the demands of reason, which are at the foundation of enlightened and civilized life.

IS *EDUCATION* A CONTESTED CONCEPT?

As long as schools exist as public institutions their aims will continue to be contested even within the most homogeneous societies; these aims are not matters of definition but of argument and policy based on the information, aspirations, priorities, needs, commitments, social conditions, and the level of education of the contestants. Can the criteria of education be contested in the same manner?

Our concept of education is ours – a tautology that is worth remembering. The native people of Canada couldn't have had it two hundred years ago, and, for the same reasons, we couldn't say that it can be found in Homer's *Odyssey*, the Bible, the Koran, or any other "holy" book. As I emphasized earlier, our concept of education today presupposes the differentiation among the various forms of knowledge and understanding through which we make sense of ourselves and the world today; it also presupposes those complex intellectual achievements and principles within each form of human inquiry. Without or outside such traditions we cannot talk about education, unless of course we are using *education* to mean *socialization*. Our ideally educated person recognizes the demands of reason within each universe of discourse and has mind and character disciplined by the standards of excellence that are embedded in them. The fact that the demands of reason are not always clear or easy to articulate does not mean that we can abandon the search for them; it simply makes our educational task more difficult or less certain. The search for understanding has only one direction; one is allowed to take alternate paths, follow different signposts, slow down, or speed up, but one cannot go back to one's unexamined beliefs and superstitions and still claim that one is engaged in the pursuit of knowledge and understanding.

The knowledge and value criteria of education serve to remind us that the intellectual achievements of humanity within which the demands of reason are embedded are not mere skills of knowing how to get along in life, nor are they doctrinal, superstitious, or mythological accounts of the world and human experience. Whatever the epistemological status of scientific theories, historical explanations, mathematical or moral claims, philosophical methods, or literary and artistic criteria, the truth is that no one can get an education without engaging in a conversation with some of the existing traditions of thought, including the controversies within these forms of human discourse. Does it make sense, then, to say that the knowledge and value criteria of education are contestable? Could one become an educated person today without acquiring some worthwhile understanding? Is there an alternative way of getting an education, outside such traditions?

One might argue that while the knowledge and value criteria of education are part of the uncontestable logical grammar of that concept they do not enable us to make all of our important educational decisions. But they assist us in making the most fundamental educational decisions; they help us to exclude from educational programs all doctrinal beliefs, superstitions, prejudices, unsupported claims, mere opinions, and all non-rational and immoral methods of dealing with the young citizens. A concept that enables us to distinguish between civilization and primitive ways of life should be deemed as one of the most valuable concepts in any language. Of course, the criteria of education don't tell us which specific disciplines, programs, and books to include in our educational programs and which methods or organizational structures we should use in order to educate the young. But, then, why should they do that? There are countless activities and experiences that have educational value and one can choose many combinations of these worthwhile pursuits in order to design an educational program. Likewise, there is a great variety of ways one can teach children successfully, so long as the teacher is knowledgeable, imaginative, caring, and committed to a vision of the good society. Our educational paradise, then, is a pluralistic one with regard to the content of education. There are many ways one can save the educational souls of citizens, young and old; unless, of course, one assumes arbitrarily that all young people should have exactly the same homogenized educational diet, that there is only one set of activities that should be included in every educational program, or that there are only certain methods, procedures, institutional provisions, and, therefore, only one process of education (i.e., schooling). As we shall see in the next chapter, our concept of education, which lies at the heart of an open society, does not require predetermined objectives, specific programs of study, or homogenized official curricula – that is what training and indoctrination require. Education requires only clear and defensible criteria of educational value, justified principles, recognized canons of inquiry, and standards of excellence, which are all embedded in countless worthwhile human achievements.

A THEORY *OF* EDUCATION AND THEORIES *IN* EDUCATION

It follows from the above that a theory of education is necessarily philosophical in character. One of the central tasks of an educational theory is to establish clear and defensible criteria of education that will demarcate the character of our educational ideal and the broad scope of the educationally worthwhile activities. These criteria are implicit in the ordinary ways we use the term education; we talk about educational, miseducational, and noneducational practices, programs, goals, functions, and institutions; we give educational reasons and arguments; we dispute the educational value of certain activities and characterize people as educated or uneducated. As I have already argued, educational engagements are normative and imply both knowledge and value criteria. A theory of education that cannot give a clear, accurate, and defensible account of these criteria will be unable to distinguish education from mere training, socialization, miseducation, indoctrination, and propaganda and should be, therefore, considered crude and worthless; it cannot guide our thoughts, judgments, and decisions when we engage in educational policymaking or practice. The reasons the discussions on the nature of educational theory have floundered are the lack of a clear and justified view of education, the tendency to confuse education with schooling or some presumed processes "in the mind," and the bewitchment of our intelligence by the scientific paradigm of theory.

As I will argue in the final chapter, our view of education as an ideal of human development is inseparable from our idea of human nature and human flourishing and is thus constitutive of our view of the good life. Consequently, a theory of education must be informed by sound theories of knowledge, value, language, and mind and must be an integral part of sound political theorizing. Since knowledge is one of the criteria of education it is necessary that a theory of education be well informed about the conditions of knowledge as well as about the various forms of understanding through which we make sense of the world and of human experience. Without a clear view of what constitutes a knowledge claim we cannot distinguish education from indoctrination, propaganda, and other forms of miseducation.

Equally important to a defensible and useful view of education is the determination of the value criterion of education. The great danger that threatens education today is the almost exclusive emphasis on the instrumental value of educational activities and the hedonistic ethic that is prevalent in our society and public schools. Particularly problematic are some technocratic and pseudoscientific perspectives of the human mind and behaviour that have distorted our view of the learner, the nature of learning and teaching, education in general, and particularly moral education.

Similarly, our theory of education will only be as sound as the theory of mind embedded in it. Our ordinary views of the mind are all metaphorical, with each metaphor giving a certain perspective of it. Some of the views of mind that have survived in the language of teaching are more or less obsolete metaphors and have misled generations of educational thinkers, policy-makers, and practitioners. "To furnish the mind with knowledge" implies that the mind is similar to an empty room; "To transmit knowledge" gives the impression that the mind is an inert receiver, while "To instill or inculcate certain beliefs" suggests that the mind is a tabula rasa. "To exercise the mind or train children's reasoning or memory" suggests that the mind consists of some kind of separate mental departments or muscles. The horticultural metaphor of mind conveys the idea that it is like a field that has been lying fallow and must be "cultivated." Some of the most influential metaphors in education, namely molding, growth, and development, are not without their severe limitations.

While it could be said, with appropriate qualifications, that education is the development of mind, it would be a mistake to consider education responsible for its genesis. As will be shown later, we acquire our minds through early socialization, not through education; education is the further development of mind. And yet, little attention has been paid by philosophers of education to the appropriate acquisitions that constitute the prerequisites of educational development; in chapter 4 we shall begin to examine those in detail.

These, then, are some of the dimensions of a serious and coherent theory of education. They provide the philosophical background against which we should make all our decisions regarding educational institutions, policies, programs, activities, and methods, and they give us the criteria of what is to count as relevant and worthwhile research for educational policy and practice. A theory of education, then, should not be confused with specific psychological or other theories concerning the best conditions of learning various subjects, the most effective means of motivating or teaching the young, the most efficient or economical institutional planning, and the like. A theory of education puts severe constraints on all such theories, and to the extent that they meet such constraints, they might be considered theories in education, i.e., theories that are relevant to educational policy and practice. Theories in education will inform us on what is conditionally possible or effective and thus they will provide the boundaries of realistic, efficient and informed educational policy and practice. Nothing of what I have said so far suggests that a theory of education is carved in stone; it must be constantly improved by the most sophisticated and refined philosophical thinking and must be a reflection of our self-awareness and humanity. When educational policy is conducted in the absence of a theory of education it is usually in the service of non-educational objectives; vague slogans or metaphors of various kinds are used in its place.

3

Can Education Have Aims?

The answer to the question "Can education have aims?" is not unlike the answer to the question "Does life have aims?" – neither of them can have aims, unless of course by *education* one means *schooling* and by *life* one means *a person's life*. And yet, the "*aims* of education," where *education* is used in its normative sense, have been debated in modern history and have been restated countless times. Today there are still some educationalists who continue to insist on the need for formulating the "aims of education," while others maintain that all such statements are useless, high-sounding vague claims that should be abandoned for the sake of clearly defined, specific curriculum objectives. In this chapter I shall attempt to demonstrate the inappropriateness of talking about "educational aims" and "objectives" and shall investigate the various functions of such statements within educational policy. Getting a clear view of education is one of the main aims of philosophy of education, and finding "the path from error to truth," as Wittgenstein suggested, is the most reliable way of achieving that end.

EDUCATION AND AIMS

As I mentioned in the previous chapter, it is an unfortunate fact about the word *education* that it has come to refer, among other things, to the institution of schooling as well as to the development of desirable states of mind and character in a person. That confusion is to some extent understandable since the public school is considered to be the only institution in our society that is committed primarily to education. The fact that *education* has variable meanings, however, should not in itself be a problem (the meaning of many words varies with different contexts), but unfortunately it is. The confusion of education with schooling is apparent in all talk about the "aims of education" or the "theory of education."

There is an obvious category mistake in the phrase "aims of education," when *education* is used in its important normative sense. It is only persons who can be said to have aims and, derivatively, human activities, programs, and institutions. Education is not in a category of things that can have aims, goals, or objectives. As R.S. Peters has argued, education is a word that encapsulates certain criteria (the knowledge and value criteria I discussed earlier) to which activities, programs, methods, or institutions must conform in order to be judged educational.[1] Thus, while it is quite appropriate to inquire about the aims of persons, activities, or institutions, it is as incorrect to ask about the aims of education as it is to ask about the aims of virtue, justice, or knowledge. "What are its aims?" is not a proper question regarding education; rather, we should be asking "What does it mean?" "What are its criteria?" or "What is its scope and value?" We will be amply rewarded by examining the logical behaviour of *aim* in its various contexts. Not only will we be gaining greater conceptual clarity and elegance, we will also avoid all the unnecessary and wasteful talk that directs our attention away toward nebulous ideas and vacuous aims.

Interestingly, the concept of *aim* behaves differently when it is predicated of persons than when it is predicated of activities or institutions. The aims (as well as the goals, objectives, aspirations) that we have may be numerous, varied, changing, realistic, or unrealistic. They are limited only by the constraints imposed on us by our own natures and the nature of the world we inhabit, including the nature of our culture and the particular contingencies of a person's life. Ideally, then, the educational aims of an individual should be limited only by the criteria of educational worthwhileness, the nature of the available educational goods, and the varying abilities, interests, and needs of the young to choose among worthwhile activities. An important corollary of the above is that, in an ideal world, educational institutions must have pluralistic aims, serving the educational interests and needs of each student. If this reasoning is correct then it follows that the onus is always on those who want to control other people's educational pursuits, to justify their actions that aim at limiting the choices of the learners.

The case is quite different with human activities. Activities are rule-governed and have specific and preferred descriptions. If I am gardening, then the facts that while I am doing so I am also exercising, getting my hands dirty, and upsetting some worms are irrelevant to the description of the activity in which I am engaged. A statement about the aims of an activity is an alternative way of describing the activity; it tells us what an activity is for and therefore what it is. Statements about the aims of an activity are definitional of the activity. The statement "The aim of teaching is to bring about learning" means the same as the statement "Teaching is an activity that aims at bringing about learning." That does not mean, of course, that there cannot be programmatic definitions of activities; some of the most interesting but controversial definitions of *teaching*, for example, are programmatic.[2] It goes without saying, of course, that even the most exhaustive enumeration of a person's aims cannot define that person.

Finally, statements about the aims of institutions are always programmatic, prescribing what institutions ought to do and, consequently, how they ought to be evaluated.[3] Only doctrinaire conservatives would maintain that such statements describe what institutions are for, and therefore what they are; a case in point is the current debate on marriage between homosexuals. The aims of an institution cannot be established with definitions; they are matters of public policy and can be subject to debate and change. It is by no means being suggested here, however, that institutions are arbitrary conventions that can be changed or abandoned at will; all that is claimed is that they are changeable. Moreover, to claim that aims statements that refer to institutions are descriptive is to overlook the important distinction between the aims of an institution and its actual functions. What an institution is *for* is what it *ought to do*, whereas what an institution *is* is what in fact it *does* or how it actually functions. While the aims of public schools are matters of public policy and are the responsibility of the policymaking body, some important functions of the schools may be largely unintentional. To maintain that statements about the aims of institutions are descriptive is to ignore the crucial distinction between the intended and unintended consequences of our decisions and actions and of the institutional arrangements we create; that distinction is surely of fundamental importance for any serious educational and social policy. The extensive literature on the "hidden curriculum" aims to draw attention to the unintended consequences of schooling.

AIMS AS SPECIFIC OBJECTIVES AND AS STANDARDS OF EXCELLENCE

There are a number of educational slogans that have been around for a long time masquerading as aims of education, and these we must deal with rather swiftly; "meeting the needs and interests of students" and "developing their potential" are among such vacuous slogans that appear regularly in statements of educational policy. In order to see how empty and misleading these slogans are all we have to do is ask: "which needs and interests?" and "potential for what?" The words *need* and *interest* can be used descriptively, referring to the felt needs and interests of students, or they can be used prescriptively, referring to their long-term worthwhile interests and needs, as decided by society. The omitted criterion in the talk about developing the students' potential is that of its educational worthwhileness. Once we add that criterion we get useless tautologies: "the aim of education is to meet the educationally worthwhile needs and interests of the young" or "to develop their educational potential." Those who resort to such mind-numbing, evasive, and dull slogans show that they have not thought seriously about the criteria of education.

In other similarly vague talk about educational aims and curriculum objectives the difference between aims and objectives has usually been misunderstood; aims are considered general and broad while objectives are regarded as detailed and specific. Aims are supposed to have implications for the whole curriculum as they are "translated" or "broken down" into specific objectives. Objectives must be "derived" from the general aims and shaped by them and when they are reached they are expected to realize these aims.

This hierarchical view of the nature of aims and objectives and their putative relationship is one of the most serious confusions in educational discourse and especially in talking about the curriculum; it has been created largely as a result of not paying attention to the actual workings of our language. The confusion becomes obvious when we examine the two different uses of the word *aim* in ordinary language; we talk about "aiming *at*" something or "aiming *for*" something.

"AIMING *AT*"

The question "What are you aiming at?" when it is asked of an army recruit, a hunter, or a teacher is a request for a specification of some precise objective; answers such as "target 13," "the large duck," or "typing sixty words a minute" specify their objectives precisely and adequately and offer a satisfactory explanation of their respective activities. The objectives we aim at in educational practice are numerous and varied: making the students feel comfortable, teaching them how to read and write, showing them how to use a computer, asking them to memorize a poem, learn the rules of grammar, logic, and good behaviour or the meanings of concepts. In ordinary circumstances the objectives aimed at by the teacher are clear, specific, and attainable and questions like "what do you mean by 'making the students feel comfortable'?" do not arise. When they do, it is usually because the objectives are unclear, unrealizable, or illegitimate and we want them restated for examination and criticism. We can conclude, then, that *aiming at* statements are about specific, determinate objectives. Objectives are nothing more than the specific things we teach, develop, cultivate, or nurture; it is when it is not clear what teachers are aiming at that it is appropriate to ask about their objectives, not when we are planning the curriculum. We can even avoid using the pretentious pseudotechnical word *objective* altogether by asking: "*What* do you plan to teach?" The answer will always be a specific skill, rule, theory, axiom, principle, and the like; "teaching objectives" is vacuous logical nonsense.

"AIMING *FOR*"

It appears that there is an important difference between the phrases *aiming at* and *aiming for*. In admonishing teachers, the school superintendent may become a little animated and exhort them to "aim for the stars" – and we know that the teachers will not misunderstand this advice by aiming the school telescope *at* the stars! Unlike specific and determinate objectives (i.e., the content, implied by *aiming at* statements), the objectives of *aiming for* statements are general and indeterminate. While the question "what are you aiming *at*?" can be answered by mentioning specific content, the question "what are you aiming *for*?" (which is usually asked of teachers, union leaders, and politicians) can be answered by providing a regulative principle or standard of excellence in accordance with which we are acting or under which we are supposed to consider and judge a specific teaching act. Responses such as "more freedom in education" or "a proper understanding of science" do not refer to specific objectives that can be aimed at and reached, or general objectives that must first be "broken down" or "translated" and then pursued; they tell us under which one of a number of possible alternative principles or norms we should perceive and evaluate certain activities. Although they are always offered as aims or goals, they are really about the regulative principles or standards that govern a person's thoughts and actions and they help us interpret and understand these actions in a certain way. Unlike specific educational objectives, these regulative principles are indeterminate and are, therefore, always in need of interpretation and defense. Typical goals we aim for are freedom, autonomy, moral character, critical thinking, open-mindedness, respect for persons, understanding, appreciating works of art, justice, the good life – all of which are general human excellences, virtues or attainments and, therefore, inseparable from certain principles or standards of appraisal. With considerable support from ordinary language, then, we can conclude that the question "What are you aiming *for*?" is a request for a characterization of a certain activity or activities; it is not simply a request for a specification of that activity, as R.S. Peters has suggested.[4]

THE "AIMS OF EDUCATION"

It appears from the above analysis that the "aims of education" that are recommended by educational policymakers are usually the things we aim *for* rather than *at*; they are not about specific content but about indeterminate perspectives, guiding principles, or standards of excellence that are always in need of interpretation and rational defense. Since education is neither a person nor an activity or institution (and therefore cannot logically be said to have aims), the net effect of claims about the "aims of education" is the inevitable programmatic narrowing of the scope of educationally worthwhile activities or their abandonment. In other words, statements about the aims of education are always selective and prescriptive; they must, therefore, be interpreted and defended by their proponents, otherwise they cannot be evaluated correctly and adequately. We can identify the following uses of such statements.

TAUTOLOGIES

One might argue that some aims statements (e.g., "The aim of education is to develop the mind – mind understood in its broadest sense") should be accepted as descriptive definitions of education (i.e., "Education is the development of the mind"). To the extent that such statements are accepted as adequate, albeit very general, definitions of education, they are tautologies, i.e., they purport to tell us what education means or is. They do that, however, in an awkward way by committing an obvious and unnecessary category mistake; as I mentioned earlier, education is not in the category of things that can have aims or objectives. It would certainly be better if such confusing expressions were eliminated altogether from our language and a serious effort was made instead to specify and defend the criteria of education and its legitimate dimensions.

EMPHASES

A more common use of "aims of education" statements is to emphasize some principle or standard that is immanent in a particular human achievement or excellence (history or science) and, in the view of the speaker or writer, has been neglected by the educational community. The statement "The aim of education is to develop critical thinking rather than mere memorizing" is such a reminder. One of the problems such slogans create is that by emphasizing one legitimate principle of educational development they overlook or de-emphasize other important dimensions. In order to repair the damage done by such statements of emphasis, then, we should have to offer an extremely long list of correctives enumerating all the other valuable educational excellences that are also worth pursuing. The corrective to the above statement of emphasis would be: "Yes, educators should try to develop critical thinking, but also the imagination of the young and their moral character, and their aesthetic sensibilities, their creative thinking, and so on." Statements of emphasis, then, not only are guilty of committing a category mistake, they also commit a sin of omission; they invariably ignore, suppress, or de-emphasize a multitude of other equally important dimensions of education.

PROGRAMMATIC DEFINITIONS (EDUCATIONAL)

Most often, "aims of education" statements, which appear to be statements of emphasis, are disguised programmatic definitions of education. Proponents of such definitions of education choose one of the above educational excellences and present it as if it were *the* necessary and sufficient condition for the application of the term. The function of such programmatic definitions is to narrow the scope of educational excellences for some purpose. The history of educational policy is a series of alternating programmatic definitions of education. We should put an end to this entire talk about "the aims of education."

PROGRAMMATIC DEFINITIONS (NON-EDUCATIONAL)
A rather pernicious use of "aims of education" statements will be found in the constitutions or policy statements of several countries, where education is considered to be primarily or exclusively a means for the realization of external ends, usually political, religious, or economic. In these cases the value criterion of education is replaced by the values of the official ideology, which determine the whole character of the enterprise. The engagement is no longer considered to be worthwhile in itself but is pursued for its instrumental value. Even seemingly innocuous statements of aims that appear in policy documents of ministries of education, such as "citizenship" or "productivity," are vague slogans in the service of the political and economic status quo; they are always interpreted by the state officials to serve their political ends, thus reducing education to a means for the achievement of external ends. In the most extreme cases we can no longer talk about education but rather about training, indoctrination, or socialization, whereas in the less extreme cases the educational systems pursue incompatible goals, i.e., they educate with some of their programs and miseducate with others. A clear example of such irreconcilable and contradictory aims can be found in the modern Greek Constitution, which states that the aim of education is "the moral, intellectual, *vocational* and *physical* education of the Greeks, the development of their *national* and *religious* conscience and their formation into free and *responsible* citizens" (my emphasis).

A general criticism of all "aims of education" statements, even when they are tautologies or emphases, is that they are nothing more than vague slogans; the criteria of what constitutes critical thinking, creativity, open-mindedness, understanding, appreciation, for example, are always context dependent and vary according to various human activities; they cannot be taught in a contextual vacuum. It is logically impossible to teach understanding or creativity in the abstract without specific content; neither can one cultivate, nurture, or exercise them as if they were independent faculties of the mind.

Whether aims of education statements are tautologies, emphases, or programmatic definitions, they are confusing and misleading. What is important for educational policy and practice is to get clear about the nature and value of education and its important dimensions. Appeals to the aims of education are idle and illusory ways of avoiding the complex tasks of selecting the educationally worthwhile subjects, skills, rules, values, and habits and the most appropriate manner of teaching them to the young. There is a very serious confusion here: it is quite appropriate to ask a teacher, "What are you aiming *at* or *for*?" because you are perplexed by what that teacher is doing; but it is inappropriate and misleading to confuse the context where we ask for clarification of a teacher's actions with the context of identifying and defending the criteria of education or the content of curriculum. The most appropriate language in educational planning is ordinary language: "We educate students by teaching them X, Y, and Z"; all references to aims and objectives are redundant, pretentious, and confusing jargon. At best *aims* statements can be used as reminders for a teacher who falls short of the demands of good teaching; one might say to such a teacher: "Don't aim merely at memorization but help the students to understand or appreciate the subject."

CURRICULUM AIMS AND OBJECTIVES

It might be argued that, although education cannot have aims or objectives, a curriculum, being a program of studies, must have aims or objectives; after all, how could there be a program without aims or objectives. A program is never without purpose. A curriculum for preparing philosophers must, logically, be different from a curriculum for preparing carpenters. Furthermore, without a precise specification of a program's objectives it is logically impossible to evaluate it.

There is no intrinsic reason why schools ought to be educational institutions; they could be institutions that train, indoctrinate, and socialize the young, which, in fact, they often are. Once, however, we decide that schools ought to operate mainly as educational institutions certain things follow: we cannot indoctrinate or merely train the future citizens in our schools. Educational institutions are expected to provide a) the prerequisites of education (which I will discuss later), b) educate by teaching the various forms of knowledge and understanding and the norms that are inherent in each form, and c) teach other useful skills and subjects that society deems worthwhile, as long as these do not violate the criteria of education or displace educationally valuable subjects.

It would probably be rare to find a book on educational curriculum that does not refer to educational aims and objectives. Although there are disagreements among curriculum writers on the nature of aims, goals, and objectives, there is near unanimity on the necessity for specifying and defending them as requirements of rational curriculum planning. Even one of the most important and careful writer on educational curriculum, Paul H. Hirst, concurs on the need for specific curriculum objectives:

> For curriculum planning to be rational, it must start with clear and *specific* objectives, and then, and only then, address itself to discovering the plan of means, the content and methods in terms of which these objectives are to be obtained. It is on this view a *logical nonsense* to pretend that a series of activities form a curriculum, or a part of a curriculum, if they are not designed to obtain specifiable *objectives.*[5]

Hirst repeatedly emphasizes his point that "there can be no curriculum without objectives" and that such objectives ought to be formulated "clearly, in realistic and operational terms."[6] His surprising suggestion is that content and methods are merely the means for developing "understanding, judgment, imagination,"[7] and many other sophisticated and "complex objectives by way of particular dispositions, types of intellectual skills, various habits of mind and the like."[8] His reason for giving such central place to objectives is that in their absence "the teacher pares down what is to be achieved to the acquisition of information and the ability to perform a number of stated operations"; instead of understanding and all the other high-level intellectual developments of mind "the result will often be the mere mastery of propositions."[9]

I want to argue that this view about the centrality of specific objectives in educational planning is wrongheaded and that its consequences have been adverse not only for curriculum but especially for our understanding of teaching and the way we have been selecting and preparing teachers for our educational institutions. How can the teacher identify and teach intellectual and moral virtues such as commitment to clarity, precision, meticulousness, elegance, honesty, kindness, openness, patience, fairness, respect for others, and the countless other virtues and dispositions that characterize the educated person? These are not subjects in the curriculum, like mathematics or physics, but are embedded in all good teaching if they are constitutive of teachers' minds and characters and are exhibited in their everyday lives and teaching activities.

The mistaken view that aims, goals, and objectives ought to be understood hierarchically, from the most general to the specific, has led to the awkward belief among curriculum "theorists" that general aims ought to be "broken down" into specific objectives. As I have argued earlier, however, the "aims of the curriculum" can be understood to be either determinate objectives, i.e., specific content, *at* which we can aim, or indeterminate regulative principles or standards of excellence that are inherent in the content of the various disciplines. We choose to teach certain subjects and the principles or standards that are immanent in them. It is meaningless, therefore, to talk about "breaking down" such guiding principles or standards of thought.

The belief that the content of the curriculum is simply a means for the development of "understanding, judgment, imagination," and other "types of intellectual skills," as Hirst and others maintain, rests on a defunct view of the mind as consisting of various discrete faculties that can be exercised and strengthened by the use of certain content.[10] This view of mind, which derives from Faculty Psychology or some version of it, is behind the current emphasis on critical thinking, problem solving, and creativity, as if these were unitary abilities or skills that could be applied universally or taught independently of their content.[11] It contradicts Hirst's own thesis that there are distinct forms of understanding, each with its own concepts and tests for truth or standards of appraisal.[12] Whatever one's views on the forms of knowledge thesis, one has to admit that our judgments and decisions and our ability to think critically or creatively are logically constitutive of the various subjects or forms of understanding. It just does not make sense to claim that a person who has learned to think critically about scientific problems will therefore think critically about moral, aesthetic, or philosophical issues about which they know nothing or very little. The rules of logic inherent in our ordinary language enable us to communicate on all sorts of ordinary issues, but they are not sufficient to enable us to think critically, imaginatively, or creatively about science, engineering, philosophy, art, and the other forms of human thought.

The alleged need for curriculum objectives, which are supposed to be independent of content, also rests on a very serious misunderstanding of our concept of knowledge. One of Hirst's arguments for the need for clear and detailed curriculum objectives is that without them teachers tend to emphasize the mere mastery of information in the form of propositions. But the reason teachers emphasize the mere mastery of propositions is not that they do not have clear and detailed objectives; it is rather that they have a poor grasp of the character and depth of the enterprise in which they are engaged, the nature, scope, and power of the subjects they teach, and the standards immanent within them. As Israel Scheffler put it:

> Attributions of knowledge are not, in typical cases, simply *descriptive* of bodies of lore or types of experience; they express *our standards, ideals, and tastes* as to the scope and proper conduct of the cognitive arts. They reflect, for example, our conceptions of truth and evidence, our estimates of the possibilities of secure belief, our preferences among alternative strategies of investigation. . . Correspondingly, education is concerned to transmit not only what we know, but our *manner of knowing*, that is, our approved standards of competence in performance, in inquiry and in intellectual criticism.[13]

What teachers need in order to fulfill their responsibilities as educators (and to avoid the mere teaching of information) is to have, first, not specific or nebulous objectives but clear and defensible criteria of educational worth that will enable them to gain an understanding of the nature and legitimate dimensions of the educational engagement and, secondly, a thorough understanding of the nature of their subject, its appropriate standards of excellence, the conflicting views on the epistemic nature of the claims made within their discipline, the possibilities, limitations, and alternatives that exist within their subject, and the ways in which it affects or is affected by developments in other subjects. We do not teach aims or objectives but only subjects and their inherent standards, ideals, and tastes. The methods of teaching, although important, are logically secondary to the above two tasks, because the nature of the educational enterprise and the particular subjects being taught put severe constraints on what should be considered appropriate and effective methods of teaching. Moreover, what are often taken to be matters of method are often moral issues having to do with the appropriate ways of teaching and treating the young; my insistence that education ought to be understood as a dialogue implies also that the most fitting methods of teaching the young are by example and by engaging them in dialogue.

There seem to be two reasons for the excessive emphasis on curriculum objectives today, both programmatic. The first is pathological and is the result of the failure to prepare well-educated and committed teachers. One can understand that statements of curriculum aims may be used occasionally to remind us of the principles that ought to guide our educational activities or of the standards inherent in the content of teaching, when they are ignored or violated in educational practice. The persistent preoccupation with aims and objectives, however, has primarily a remedial function; it purports to provide poorly educated teachers with some procedures that will enable them to handle their subject matter in a standardized manner that usually leads to a false sense of security and professional authority. Talk about "teacher-proof curriculum" and other mindless slogans are extreme examples of the wrongheaded approach to the complex issue of determining the worthwhile content of education and preparing teachers properly. The serious problem with this short-term remedial strategy is that it has failed to address the real problem of how to prepare teachers for our educational institutions and ultimately has perpetuated and exacerbated that problem. By concentrating on the wrong target of remediation for a long time this strategy has become part of the problem. The preoccupation with predetermined objectives is certainly antithetical to the dialogical character of education about which I spoke earlier; it ignores the potentially valuable interests of students and emphasizes the monological, didactic, and controlling modes of teaching – objectives are, as a matter of fact, determined by the curriculum planner or teacher and usually disregard the interests of students.

The second reason for bringing objectives into the curriculum is political and is motivated by two different concerns. The first has to do with the perceived need for trained citizens who serve the technological needs of a competitive world. Talk about objectives is appropriate when one wants to train people who will produce a clearly pre-specified determinate outcome, as in typing or assembly work. These are linear, product-oriented programs designed for predetermined purposes. My great concern is that narrow professional training is gradually becoming a substitute for education. I suspect that the most serious threat to education in the future will come not only from indoctrinatory policies and practices of closed and illiberal regimes but also from the training needs of an increasingly competitive technological world. When specific prescribed objectives and rules, rather than criteria of educational worthwhileness, guide the curriculum, the result is control of the minds of teachers and students and the impoverishment of the whole educational endeavour.

Another politically motivated reason for emphasizing curriculum objectives is to make it serve specific political ends. The displacement of History and Geography from the curriculum, for example, by Social Studies was not an educational decision. The political objectives of the various versions of that course that one finds in North America vary from the most explicit form of indoctrination to the most confused forms of socialization. The frequent claim that education is the socialization of the young, which figures prominently in the traditional textbooks in sociology of education, has the same reactionary political origin. As will be argued later, equating education with socialization is one of the most serious and widespread confusions about the nature of education; the result of having been socialized is that one has usually learned to be a passive participant in a way of life – conforming to the rules of the group and meeting the expectations of the significant others in one's society. The result of having been educated, on the other hand, is that one has come to gain a critical understanding of oneself and the world in which one lives through the concepts and methods provided by the various disciplines.

The purpose of this chapter has been to clarify the logic of *aims* and *objectives* and to draw attention to the serious confusions about them in talking about the curriculum. As often happens, here, too, conceptual confusion reflects a misunderstanding of the phenomena under consideration and a wrong approach to the practical problem of preparing teachers for educational institutions.

The insistence on the putative curriculum objectives in teacher education has shifted the emphasis away from the study of the nature of education and the disciplines of thought and action that are central to the understanding of ourselves and the world we live in. Instead of concentrating on developing clear and defensible criteria of educational worthwhileness in teachers and improving their educational judgment, many teacher trainers have been offering them specific rules and recipes and nebulous objectives. They have misunderstood the nature of knowledge by reducing it to mere information and skills and then attempting to teach the diverse standards inherent in different subjects in a contextual vacuum – which is the same as hunting educational unicorns.

What we need for our educational institutions are teachers who have a clear vision of education, are exemplars of all the intellectual and moral virtues, and care about the proper development of the young and the quality of life in their society;

as I will argue later, the most appropriate and effective ways of teaching are by example and by dialogue that motivates and engages the minds of the young. The methods of teaching, as I argued earlier, are logically derivative and secondary to the above tasks, while talk about objectives distorts the nature of educational goods and impoverishes our lives.

PART TWO

The Prerequisites of Education and Dialogue, the Criteria of Indoctrination, and the Educational Dimensions of Human Nature

4

The Prerequisites of Education

Any explanation has its foundation in training. (Educators ought to remember this.)

Wittgenstein[1]

The extensive discussion of the nature of education in the first part of this book was necessary because we must have a clear view of the character of our educational ideal in order to choose the content, methods, and institutional arrangements that are appropriate to it. The fact that people may disagree about the content of education does not refute or weaken this claim. Proposed educational programs may be broad or narrow, progressive or conservative; whatever their character or scope they must be based on some defensible view of education if they are to be considered serious educational proposals. Without a clear conception of education we cannot know what might be distinctive of educational policy, institutions, reasons, values, programs, goals, or problems. Educational policy that is not based on a clear, coherent, and defensible view of education is usually chameleonic, serving the interests of the political and economic status quo.

A second, equally important reason for the need to get clear about the concept of education is that such an understanding is necessary for demarcating and determining the character and scope of the prerequisites of educational development as well as the methods that are appropriate for teaching them to the young. Being educated is a complex and sophisticated achievement that has its prerequisites in the form of beliefs, attitudes, dispositions, rules, skills, and the like. Our criteria of education put some clear constraints on what constitute appropriate educational prerequisites. The problem in educational theory and practice is that the distinction between education and its prerequisites is usually ignored. When it is hinted at by philosophers of education, it is casual, unclear, and inaccurate, whereas when it is totally ignored it often renders education a useless all-embracing concept more or less synonymous with socialization. The purpose of this chapter is to show the legitimacy and fundamental importance of the distinction between education and its prerequisites. As I will argue later these prerequisites require ways of teaching that are distinctly different from the sophisticated intellectual acts that are appropriate for other complex educational tasks.

THE IMPORTANCE OF THE DISTINCTION BETWEEN EDUCATION AND ITS PREREQUISITES

Talk about the prerequisites of education is as old as education itself. Rationalists like Plato see prerequisites usually as desirable habits, dispositions, and beliefs that must be established in the young as early as possible in order for them to serve as handmaids of reason. The prerequisites are supposed to be inculcated by training and habituation, whereas educational development is to be obtained through the diverse and sophisticated operations of reason. This way of thinking about prerequisites, however, creates an apparent paradox: how is it possible for habits that are presumed to be deprived of reason to be prerequisites of the development of reason?[2] I will try to show later that the rationalists were justified in talking about the prerequisites of education but wrong about the nature and scope of these prerequisites.

Here, I first want to defend the legitimacy and importance of the distinction between education and its prerequisites, which has been blurred by several educational theorists old and new.[3] I won't discuss all the reasons that led various educationalists to ignore this distinction; I will only mention one that could arguably be supported by ordinary language. There is that general descriptive use of the word education that refers to all the learning or experiences of a person as in the phrase "The education of Alexander the Great." The distinction between education and its prerequisites here disappears but so also does the importance of the word education for educational theory and practice. One does not have to be a conservative Platonist in order to be concerned with the importance of early training; most educational theorists have talked about the need for establishing appropriate habits, attitudes, and beliefs in the young.

It is part of the human condition that we do not begin our lives like Rodin's *The Thinker*, capable of performing the refined intellectual acts of educated adults. If education implies worthwhile knowledge and understanding then the very young cannot be educated without first acquiring its appropriate prerequisites.

EARLIER VIEWS ABOUT THE NATURE OF PREREQUISITES

One of the reasons old views about the prerequisites of educational development are not satisfactory is that they lack a clear view of education. As I mentioned earlier, if education is understood as the systematic socialization of the young, then the distinction between education and its prerequisites becomes irrelevant, and, since socialization means conformity to the existing values, beliefs, and traditions of society, it is impossible to talk about prerequisites. Furthermore, socialization may vary from one society to another whereas the prerequisites of educational development, as will be argued later, are common and stable. The distinction between primary and secondary socialization that sociologists make, although similar in some respects, is not the same as the one between education and its prerequisites.

A clear and defensible view of education, however necessary, is not sufficient to guarantee an equally clear and adequate view of the character and scope of its prerequisites. Most references to the prerequisites in educational literature are vague and unsatisfactory; mention is usually made of habit, tradition, proper rearing, and the need to control and train the young so that they acquire certain beliefs, norms, and attitudes. As far as I know no other contemporary writer has come as close to determining the nature and importance of the prerequisites of educational development as R.S. Peters. In one of his early essays Peters makes it clear that children are "outsiders" with regard to a rational moral life that requires reflective application of moral principles, that the giving of reasons has very little effect on young children, and that "they can and must enter the palace of Reason through the courtyard of Habit and Tradition." Furthermore, he agrees with Aristotle that "children gradually acquire these desirable forms of life by some on-the-spot apprenticeship system."[4]

Peters's strategy for resolving the apparent paradox in moral education, presumably created by Aristotle's emphasis on both habit and reason, is through his analysis of the concept of habit, which shows that not all habits are performed mechanically "out of habit" and therefore there is no necessary conflict between habit and reason. Thus the potentially dangerous confrontation between reason and habit comes to a happy end with the final triumph of reason. The conflict wasn't real; there was only an apparent paradox and thus Peters continues to remain "a staunch supporter of a rationally held and intelligently applied moral code."[5] Like many other philosophers, Peters seems confident that reason can penetrate the foundations of all our thinking and acting, that is, the prerequisites of our educational development. He recognizes that habits may be developed in an unthinking or mechanical manner as a result of ignorance, accident, or lack of care, but, in principle, they are not beyond the pale of reason. The prerequisites of our educational development, then, can be subjected to critical examination in accordance with the appropriate canons of reasoning and can be brought into the luminous domain of reason.[6] What I will argue later in this chapter is that the prerequisites of educational development are coextensive with the foundations of all our thinking and acting with reason and that they cannot be established as a result of rational examination and criticism by either the immature child or the autonomous and rational adult; with regard to the prerequisites of education we are all perennial children.

Peters comes closer to identifying the domain of the prerequisites of education in his later essay "What Is an Educational Process?"[7] where he makes the important distinction between educational and non-educational "processes." The former include teaching and other forms of rational engagement, whereas among the latter are informal ways of "picking up" tastes, manners, or attitudes without any intellectual engagement. Peters does not say much about these acquisitions and makes no effort to demarcate, characterize, and categorize them, although he does admit that some of them are very worthwhile. Since they do not involve the intellectual acts that educational activities require, Peters finds it difficult to consider them as educational tasks either for the student or the teacher. Those worthwhile things that we pick up or acquire without deliberation or criticism are what I want to examine in the remainder of this chapter.

THE FOUNDATIONS OF OUR THOUGHT

Within our Western philosophical tradition talk about the prerequisites of educational development – i.e., the bedrock of all our thinking and acting with reason – is problematic. Consider, for example, Plato's "divided line" in the *Republic* or his emphasis on the development of desirable habits in the young before they enter the age of reason. One needs his fanciful metaphysics in order to provide a contrived account for the emergence of reason out of mere habits and beliefs. How could his criteria of rationality, which exist at a higher level of cognition, depend on or even be related to mere opinions or habits?

Other notable attempts to provide rational foundations for our thoughts have also been disappointing. Hume's search for a rational foundation of human understanding ended with nothing but "custom" or mere "sentiment." He concluded: "we have, therefore, no choice left but betwixt a false reason and none at all. For my part, I know not what ought to be done in the present case."[8] His search for the rational justification of knowledge ended in frustration and disappointment.

Immanuel Kant followed a different strategy with regard to the foundations of knowledge. Kant's basic premise is that, since we cannot help making use of the bottom level features of knowledge (especially causal inference), we ought to accept them as rational. What is needed is *not* an objective justification of these bottom level features but rather an inquiry into what these features are and how they serve to structure human knowledge.[9] The foundations of our knowledge, that is, "the categories of the understanding," are the objective conditions of human experience. "They are fundamental concepts by which we think objects in general for appearances, and have therefore *a priori* objective validity. This is exactly what we desired to prove."[10] Contrary to Hume, Kant believed that he could offer a rational account of the epistemological foundations of our knowledge. As we shall see later these broad categories are part of the prerequisites but they do not have the a priori epistemological or ontological status that Kant assumed.

In Wittgenstein's later work we find a most promising radical transformation of the classical notion of the foundations of knowledge. Unlike Hume he finds it odd that there should be justification for all levels of knowledge. No explanations can be given for the foundations of our understanding, only descriptions, says Wittgenstein. "Giving grounds...justifying the evidence, comes to an end; – but the end is not certain propositions' striking us immediately as true, i.e., it is not a kind of *seeing* on our part; it is our *acting* which lies at the bottom of the language-game."[11] "Justification by experience," he says, "comes to an end. If it did not, it would not be justification."[12] His method is not to demonstrate the groundlessness of the rock bottom of our knowledge and understanding but to show or reveal it.

> If anyone said that information about the past could not convince him that something would happen in the future, I should not understand him. One might ask: What do you expect to be told then? What sort of information do you call

> a ground for such a belief? What do you call "conviction"? In what kind of way do you expect to be convinced? – If *these are* not grounds, then what are grounds? – If you say these are not grounds, then you must surely be able to state what must be the case for us to have the right to say that there are grounds for our assumption.[13]

The attempt to discover the foundations of induction is comparable to the primitive supposition that the Earth must rest on something, though of course no support proves satisfactory, since each would have to rest on something else. We can base one thought on other thoughts but not on thinking itself.[14]

THE ELEMENTS COMPRISING THE RIVERBED

We do not decide to hold these rock-bottom propositions, which constitute the foundations of all our thinking, as true or justified; we acknowledge them in the worldview we inherit as well as in our various ways of acting. "Our mistake is to look for an explanation where we ought to look at what happens as a 'proto-phenomenon.' That is, where we ought to have said: *this language-game is played*."[15] All doubting, arguing, and criticizing presuppose trust in what Wittgenstein calls "riverbed propositions" – a trust that is prelogical, primitive, animal. At the level of the hard bedrock we find not only propositions of logic but also certain pseudo-empirical and methodological propositions, such as the belief in the uniformity of nature (that is, the justification of the inductive argument). In addition, we find here some primordial concepts: "The concept of an experience: similar to that of an event, process, state, thing, fact, description, report. Here, I mean, we stand on the hard bedrock, which lies deeper than all special methods and language-games."[16] Beyond the hard bedrock there are other riverbed propositions (that I would like to call "ordinary certainties") that "stand fast" for us:

> I believe that I have forebears, and that every human being has them....I believe that the earth is a body on whose surface we move and that it no more suddenly disappears or the

> like than any other solid body: this table, this house, this tree, etc. If I wanted to doubt the existence of the earth long before my birth, I should have to doubt all sorts of things that stand fast for me.[17]

Finally, there is the multitude of complex, subtle, intricate language games that we all acquire as we grow up within our human communities: describing, giving orders, asking, swearing, lying, telling stories, reporting dreams, confessing motives, forming and testing a hypothesis, and the like. Later, I will revisit all these prerequisites and examine them more systematically.

THE NATURE OF THE RIVERBED

Language games, which are extensions of the more primitive kind of human behaviour,[18] together with the other riverbed propositions, constitute the prerequisites of all our knowledge and experience. They are epistemologically and developmentally prior to all sophisticated "higher"-level uses of language. As I have argued elsewhere, "They are....the indispensable ground of the most sophisticated thinking."[19]

It is important for the argument of this chapter that we get clear about the nature of these riverbed propositions that we trust – like Wittgenstein, I do not say "must trust." In addition to the metaphors already mentioned, Wittgenstein in *On Certainty* also talks about them as the "axis,"[20] the "scaffolding,"[21] and the "hinges"[22] of all our thoughts, judgments, arguments, language, and actions. They are the elements that constitute the "unmoving foundation"[23] that we inherit without the possibility of explaining, demonstrating, doubting, or justifying. They are "fossilized,"[24] given the stamp of incontestability, and "shunted onto an unused siding."[25] The groundlessness of the riverbed propositions, however, does not mean that they are irrational, hasty, or superficial assumptions or hypotheses. Instead, they determine for us what is the axis or the hinges on which all our arguments and hypotheses turn. They are "the inherited background against which (we) distinguish between true and false."[26]

HUMANITY'S NATURAL HISTORY OR FORM OF LIFE

Although Wittgenstein's method reminds us of Kant's transcendental argument it does not lead to any a priori categories but to what he called "forms of life." "What has to be accepted, the given, is – so one could say – *forms of life*."[27] The notion of a "form of life" (or humanity's "natural history"), so central to Wittgenstein's later philosophy, is not defined anywhere by him; it is one of those things that can only be revealed or shown to be there. It is used by Wittgenstein to refer to shared patterns of human activity, behavioural and linguistic, that are beyond justification and doubt. Human beings feel pain, grief, and joy and express themselves in certain characteristic ways. Our groundless form of life sets both our limits and our possibilities. All attempts to justify, refute, confirm, doubt, or disconfirm presuppose a trust in this primitive substratum.

It is part of human beings' natural history that they speak a language and can perform a great variety of language games; it is a given about human beings that they are in broad agreement not only about definitions and judgments but also about corresponding behaviour. We do not begin our lives with doubting or any other form of thinking but with the certainty of various human activities and the language games that are embedded in our form of life. "But that means I want to conceive it (certainty) as something that lies beyond being justified or unjustified; as it were, as something animal."[28] And again later: "I want to regard man here as an animal; as a primitive being to which one grants instinct but not ratiocination. As a creature in a primitive state. Any logic good enough for a primitive means of communication needs no apology from us. Language did not emerge from some kind of ratiocination."[29]

Wittgenstein's repeated references to our "animal" or "primitive" nature are meant literally. "The squirrel," he says, "does not infer by induction that it is going to need stores next winter as well. And no more do we need a law of induction to justify our actions or our predictions."[30] Logic and induction, then, are not the result of ratiocination, because all ratiocination presupposes them. Consider also the primitive nature of induction in cases where we experience fear. "The character of the belief in the uniformity of nature can perhaps be seen most clearly in the case in which we fear what we expect. Nothing could induce me to put my hand into a flame – although after all it is *only in the past* that I have burnt myself."[31] "The belief that fire will burn me is of the same kind as the fear that it will burn me."[32] "I shall get burnt if I put my hand in the fire: that is certainty. That is to say: here we see the meaning of certainty. (What it amounts to, not just the meaning of the word 'certainty.'"[33] "A man would fight for his life not to be dragged into the fire. No induction. Terror. That is, as it were, part of the substance of the belief."[34]

At the foundation of all ratiocination there are certain primal ways of acting and all our language games depend on them. "It is a help here to remember that it is a primitive reaction to tend, to treat the part that hurts when someone else is in pain... But what is the word 'primitive' meant to say here? presumably that this sort of behavior is *pre-linguistic*: that a language game is based *on it,* that it is the prototype of a way of thinking and not the result of thought."[35] Wittgenstein quotes Goethe approvingly: "In the beginning was the deed."[36]

LANGUAGE AND BEHAVIOUR

Of particular interest is what Wittgenstein says about the relationship between ordinary language and various human activities. Our language does not have its origin in some kind of pre-linguistic thinking; it is "an extension of primitive behavior. (For our *language-game* is behavior)."[37] We cannot separate thinking from man's activities "for the thinking is not an accompaniment of the work, anymore than of thoughtful speech."[38] "I really want to say that scruples in thinking begin with (have their roots in) instinct." Or again: "a language-game does not have its origin in *consideration*. Consideration is part of a language-game."[39] "What makes something a word of 'approval' or an expression of 'encouragement,'" says Derek Phillips "is the language-game and the form of life in which it appears." "We don't start from certain words," says Wittgenstein, "but from certain occasions and activities." This means that words and language cannot be understood and characterized independently of certain occasions, activities, circumstances or "forms of life" in which they are used.[40] Our words then are context-bound and this context – consisting of gestures, facial expressions, tone of voice, and the like – is not related to the language game merely contingently: it is part of the language game. Our language games are embedded in certain activities, occasions, situations, and customs. "All testing, all confirmation and disconfirmation of a hypothesis takes place already within a system. And this system....belongs to the *essence* of what we call an argument. The system is not so much the *point of departure*, as the *element in which arguments have their life*."[41] Derek Phillips argues that:

> one must understand gestures, smiles and so on, before one can understand a language....We know that children do learn the meaning of some gestures and signs – smiling, anger – before they acquire language. Unless there are some similarities between the non-verbal behavior of an individual and those whose language he is trying to learn and understand, the understanding and translation of that language would prove impossible.[42]

What is being suggested here is that in our form of life, language and thought merge with our behaviour and with the world. Or, as Wittgenstein said: "The *speaking* of language is part of an activity, or of a form of life." And if this point is correct, as I think it is, a lot of the things that have been said about education and moral education in particular are seriously lacking.

OUR RIVERBED BELIEFS AS CRITERIA OF RATIONALITY

The riverbed beliefs that form our world picture constitute the system of reference that defines our world: "it is the inherited background against which I distinguish between true and false."[43] It is, therefore, epistemologically prior because this is where we get the criteria, principles, rules, and norms for our arguments, hypotheses, and doubts. It is a continuing debate whether and to what extent the riverbed of our thought changes. Wittgenstein himself says:

> the river-bed of thoughts may shift. But I distinguish between the movement of the water on the river-bed and the shift of the bed itself though there is not a sharp division of the one from the other....And the bank of that river consists partly of hard rock, subject to no alteration or only to an imperceptible one, partly of sand, which now in one place now in another gets washed away or deposited.[44]

It seems to me that the stability of the riverbed depends on what we put in it; as I shall try to show later, that cannot be an arbitrary matter of preference. For example, "I no longer believe in the uniformity of nature" is an intelligible utterance that renders all further human experience unintelligible. That certainly cannot be the case with the statement "I no longer believe in God, miracles, or the hereafter."

Commitment to riverbed propositions is not a matter of choice or preference. In *On Certainty* Wittgenstein appeals at least fourteen times to the reasonable person who may have all sorts of doubts – but not about the riverbed beliefs. It is only the "insane," "mad," "demented," "idiotic," and "halfwits"[45] who would express doubt about such propositions and their doubt would be hollow, senseless, and without consequences.[46] Doubting that the Earth existed before one's birth or believing that one does not have forebears is not making a mistake, it is a sign of mental illness; one makes a mistake only within a system of reference.

What, then, of people who have different systems of reference and different worldviews from ours, as is the case with some extreme religious fundamentalists? Do these other worldviews constitute a challenge to our views? Since this issue will be discussed later (see chapter 6) I shall deal with it here only briefly. The onus is always on the person who claims that a certain belief belongs to the riverbed to show that it actually does. Belief or disbelief in doctrines or superstitions, for example, is not a criterion of rationality and can be challenged, whereas the questioning of riverbed beliefs is a sign of mental disturbance. Doctrines, superstitions, opinions, and even hypotheses or theories are not the sort of things that could belong to the riverbed because they can all be doubted, accepted, modified, or rejected. There can be alternatives to all of them, whereas there are no alternatives to our riverbed beliefs. Since our riverbed beliefs are presupposed by all of the above, they are not at the same epistemic level with them. Finally, as I shall argue later, riverbed beliefs are acquired or inherited without any thinking, whereas doctrines, hypotheses, theories, and so on are learned.[47]

What can be said about these real or hypothetical people whose world pictures and frames of reference are radically different from ours is that there is "an enormous gulf between us," that we are "on an entirely different plane,"[48] or that we "feel ourselves intellectually very distant" from them.[49] It seems clear to me that, most often but not always, such "gulfs" or "distances" are created because of spurious riverbed beliefs – such as doctrines, prejudices, or superstitions – that are established artificially in the minds of the very young as though they were part of the hard bedrock. There is absolutely nothing in human experience that necessitates the doctrine of the infallibility of the pope, whereas everything in human experience presupposes the law of induction or the belief in the existence of physical objects. All the beliefs I mentioned earlier as belonging to the hard bedrock of our riverbed are universal and they unite us. Doctrines and superstitions, on the other hand, are always parochial and they divide us.

It has long been a cornerstone of liberalism that more education would reduce interpersonal and international conflict and lead to better understanding and a more cooperative and peaceful world. What I have said above reinforces what we already know from experience, namely, that such optimism has been exaggerated. One of the many reasons for this failure is that when children come to school they already have a frame of reference in place; and another reason is that indoctrination and propaganda in various forms and degrees continue to establish, promote, and maintain spurious riverbed beliefs in most citizens. It seems to me that we have not paid enough attention to the fact that certain ways of life are inimical to educational development, dialogical relationships, international cooperation, and peace. Rational arguments and relevant evidence will convince those with whom we share the same frame of reference, the same prerequisites. When educational policy neglects the establishment of the proper prerequisites of educational development it is unrealistic and utopian. Talk about the prerequisites of education also suggests that we must think carefully about those aspects of our culture that facilitate desirable human development and those that hinder it. It is the everyday activities, interactions, customs, and commitments of a community that facilitate or frustrate the work of educational institutions. The work of educators will be successful to the extent that there is a shared background or frame of reference between them and their students. An adequate educational policy therefore cannot ignore those aspects of culture that may facilitate, undermine, or distort the prerequisites of education.

LEARNING AND ACQUISITION

Of equal importance and closely connected to the above points is what Wittgenstein says about the way we acquire the whole riverbed of our thought. In *Zettel* he states without further elaboration: "We are here describing a language-game that *we cannot learn*."[50] What he means is that given the foundational status of language games and other riverbed beliefs, it is obvious that these enabling beliefs constituting the framework of our thinking cannot be learned. They belong to "our whole system of verification. This system is something that a human being acquires by means of observation and instruction. I intentionally do not say 'learns.'"[51] The distinction that Wittgenstein makes here between "acquisition" and "learning" has very important consequences for our thinking about education in general but more specifically about teaching.

Learning requires prior experience and involves some form of thinking while acquisition of riverbed beliefs does not because it cannot. Unlike the understanding of knowledge claims, arguments, hypotheses, and theories, the acquisition of bedrock beliefs does not allow the use of the intellectual acts of explaining, doubting, justifying, etc.; such acts are inappropriate and ineffective for establishing the riverbed of our thought. Yet these foundational propositions are teachable and they must be taught as prerequisites to all sophisticated educational engagements. The child acquires these prerequisites, says Wittgenstein, not by explanation but by training: "The child learns by believing the adult. Doubt comes after belief."[52] Language games are possible only if one trusts something; they do not start with doubt but with certainty.

We teach the prerequisites by putting children in our way of doing things; they acquire the framework of their thinking by means of examples and by practice, not by intellectual demonstrations, definitions, or sermons. This means that children must be participants in a form of life in order to acquire the prerequisites – not mere spectators or listeners. In the following passage from *On Certainty* Wittgenstein illustrates the difference between the two kinds of teaching:

> How do I explain the meaning of "regular," "uniform," "same" to anyone? – I shall explain these words to someone who, say, only speaks French by means of the corresponding French words. But if a person has not yet got the *concepts*, I shall teach him to use the words by means of *examples* and by *practice*. – And when I do this I do not communicate less to him than I know myself....I do it, he does it after me; and I influence him by expressions of agreement, rejection, expectation, encouragement. I let him go his way, or hold him back; and so on. Imagine witnessing such teaching. None of the words would be explained by means of itself; there would be no logical circle.[53]

The standard discussions of the concept of teaching by philosophers of education limit it almost exclusively to the sophisticated intellectual acts that professionally trained teachers perform – as if we didn't teach riverbed beliefs, habits, dispositions, and attitudes to the very young and the learning-disabled. Teaching is one of the most ordinary polymorphous activities and permeates all human societies and institutions from the nuclear family to the university graduate school. We all teach others in many ways as we interact with them within our diverse social roles. The content of teaching does not consist only of those intellectual acts that are found predominantly in the educated person's quiver; it consists first of all of an enormous number of the bedrock beliefs that form the foundations of intellectual development and are therefore the prerequisites of all educational development. It would seem appropriate to refer to this early teaching as initiation into a form of life in contrast to the rational engagement that involves the intricate intellectual acts and presupposes the former. It seems to me that our ordinary locutions "learning *to*" and "teaching *to*" refer at least in part to those habits, dispositions, attainments, and attitudes that constitute the prerequisites of education. A conception of teaching that omits the prerequisites of educational development must be deemed seriously lacking; it narrows both the teaching practice as well as the study of teaching itself.[54]

RIVERBED PROPOSITIONS AND MORAL PRINCIPLES

Among the riverbed propositions that constitute the bedrock of our thoughts are countless language games such as describing, questioning, reporting, commanding, expressing approval or disapproval, promising, lying, apologizing, expressing regret, thanking, cursing, greeting, etc. As I mentioned earlier, those do not have their origin in our thinking but in primordial instincts and reactions such as experiencing fear, anger, grief, aiding a person who is in pain, and the like. A language game, says Wittgenstein, "is not based on grounds. It is not reasonable (or unreasonable). It is there – like our life."[55]

What I want to maintain here is that the principles of morality that are rooted in our acquired virtues occupy a position akin to riverbed beliefs with regard to our moral development and moral life and that they ought to be taught in a similar manner, i.e., by means of examples and by practice; examples, practice, and training are not mere contingent aids to rational moral development but the very foundation of moral education. This position is in disagreement with prevailing rationalist views on moral education that emphasize exclusively moral dilemmas, personal choice, and critical thinking and thus neglect the foundations of moral development. Just as there are methodological propositions as well as propositions in the form of empirical propositions that constitute the frame of reference for our thinking about the world and ourselves, so there are similar propositions that constitute the rules of relevance for our moral life. We do not choose, doubt, or justify the former or the latter because there are no alternatives to either of them; we are born into them and we simply acknowledge them by what we say and do. No one ever chooses one's own moral code at birth, although we can and must make many choices and changes within it later under particular circumstances. We acknowledge our moral principles just as we acknowledge the rest of the riverbed of our thought and action. Consider, for example, Wittgenstein's example in his "A Lecture on Ethics,"[56] where we find it odd to say to a person who behaves heinously: "Ah, then that's all right to behave like a beast!" We say, instead: "You ought to want to behave better." Compare that episode with the one where we say to a poor tennis player, "But it is all right not to be a champion." We would certainly feel very distant from a person who did not make the distinction between morality and skill – just as we feel we are on a different plane from a person who believes in magic or takes mythology literally.

Like Aristotle, Wittgenstein appeals repeatedly to the reasonable person who may have doubts about many things but not about riverbed beliefs. Reasonable persons do not have doubts about fundamental moral principles either, although occasionally they may fall short of them. "In certain circumstances a man cannot make a *mistake*."[57] The person who questions riverbed propositions is demented or crazy, while a person who does not recognize moral principles as binding is considered a psychopath. In both cases we are dealing with serious mental disturbances, not with mistakes. "In order to make a mistake, a man must already judge in conformity with humanity."[58] The riverbed propositions and the moral principles are criteria of rationality for their respective domains.

How Do We Acquire Fundamental Moral Principles?

It is precisely because we cannot doubt or choose our moral principles that we do not learn them either; we acquire them without thinking, the same way we acquire all our rock-bottom beliefs. "The child learns by believing the adult. Doubt comes *after* belief."[59] But we do not acquire them in any direct way. "I do not explicitly learn the propositions that stand fast for me. I can *discover* them subsequently like the axis around which a body rotates."[60]

Rationalist writers on moral education overlook the crucial fact that moral principles, like other riverbed beliefs, are embedded in shared human activities and cannot exist outside of a social context. We do not learn the meaning of a word in general but always in some context where the word is doing a specific job. As we acquire various language games we also learn the grammar implicit in our mother tongue; nobody learns the grammar first. We do not teach the principle of respect for persons, simpliciter; we teach the child by means of numerous real examples the differences between persons and objects, persons and animals, as well as the appropriate ways in which to treat people in specific instances or contexts. We begin our moral lives not with catechism or sophisticated lectures on our duties and obligations, but as apprentices, that is, as participants engaged in a form of life. I do not think there is a more profound and insightful statement on this matter than the one we find in Aristotle's *Nichomachean Ethics*:

> But the virtues we get by first *exercising them*, as also happens in the case of the arts as well. For the things we have to learn before we can do them, we learn by *doing* them, e.g., men become builders by building and lyre players by playing the lyre; so do we become just by doing just acts, temperate by doing temperate acts, brave by doing brave acts... by doing the acts that we do *in our transactions with other persons* we become just or unjust, and by doing the acts that we do in the presence of danger, and by habituating ourselves to feel fear and confidence, we become brave or cowardly.... It

> makes no small difference then, whether we form habits of one kind or another from our very youth; it makes a great difference or rather *all the difference....*"[61]

Wittgenstein gives the example mentioned earlier, of how the practice of apprenticeship works: "I do it, he does it after me; and I influence him by expressions of agreement, rejection, expectation, encouragement."[62] The question, then, is not one of developing some kind of presuppositionless moral reasoning in a contextual vacuum or in a contrived setting, because moral reasoning is parasitic on its groundless prerequisites and inseparable from its behavioural components and specific context. Doubt comes after belief, and so does every other form of reasoning. The problem is how to establish in the young the desirable dispositions, habits, virtues, and attitudes that will form the system of reference for their further development. There is a great difference between the child who is in the process of acquiring various concepts and an adult who learns a second language. The rationalists' talk about children's moral upbringing assumes that children are like sophisticated English gentry learning French.

One example of such a rationalist philosopher of moral education is John Wilson, who believes that all our moral convictions are capable of rational inspection and justification. There is no place in his theory for the kind of nonrational foundations that Wittgenstein talks about, and there is no moral community. There are only contingent preconditions that may facilitate moral reasoning in the young. With regard to the content of moral education Wilson says:

> It seems to me wise to present few, if any, items of content as definitively proven or known to be true. I am not here saying either (a) that there are not a great many such items which in fact *are* true and *can* (if we use the right methodology) be shown to be so, nor (b) that we should not present items of content at all. I am saying that we should present them as and for what they are, that is, as moral beliefs, more or less widely subscribed to, which merit inspection and verification in the light of the proper methodology.[63]

Wilson recognizes that one does not give lectures on moral reasoning to "very insecure, unloved pupils, incapable of paying much sustained attention to anything sophisticated." Such children "might rather need to be hugged and cuddled, to interact in simple ways with other children....On the other hand, for those children who already had enough security, determination, ability to defer gratification, and so on, but who were simply *ignorant* about the procedures that should govern moral thought and action, some *direct* teaching about these might profitably appear as both the *first* and the *most important* thing to do."[64]

In these two paragraphs Wilson introduces unwarranted dichotomies with serious practical consequences for moral education. Consider first the implausibility of his first suggestion: that we should offer to the young few (if any) "items of content" as known to be true – as if children were solitary creatures growing up in a social vacuum. Are we to postpone moral training until the ability to reason morally appears miraculously? Do we need to prove to the young that they should not hurt other people, and how do we show it to be "true"? Within Wilson's view of moral education, how does one talk about the development of virtues or of a person's character if everything that a person thinks or does requires his methodological scrutiny? How often and under what circumstances do we, as moral agents or as football players, actors, musicians and painters, appeal to the rules that govern our actions – if we can ever formulate such rules clearly and adequately?

Wilson here appears to be an unrepentant dualist. He recognizes that an unloved or insecure child might need to be hugged and cuddled sometimes, but he does not consider these actions as proper ingredients of moral upbringing; they are contingent external aids that might make the child morally educable. When reason comes – and here Wilson agrees with Plato –it will find allies in these lowly modes of behaviour. But the question remains for Plato as it does for Wilson: how can this humble behaviour of cuddling prepare the child for sophisticated moral reasoning? Wilson, like Peters before him, has been led into an unnecessary paradox; but since paradoxes are not part of the furniture of the world we cannot accept his views. It is also useful to be reminded of Wittgenstein's warnings against the craving for generality and his call to pay attention to the particular. "To obey a rule, to make a report, to give an order, to play a game of chess, are *customs* (uses, institutions)."[65] Obeying a rule or a principle, like other language games, is a shared practice that cannot be understood and characterized independently of certain circumstances, activities, and occasions in which it is used; it is context-bound. Learning a moral rule is a matter of degree and depends on our experiences; our understanding broadens like an expanding circle, it is not like a sudden and complete revelation. We learn to be trusting, sensitive, caring, kind, cooperative, polite, and gracious persons not as a result of certain propositions striking us as true but by gradually extending our sympathies to more and more people as we participate in a certain form of life. It would be extraordinary if children could learn the principle of respect for persons without countless real examples under suitable circumstances. Once again, it is our acting that lies at the bottom of all our language games, not some private, clear, and distinct Cartesian ideas or principles. The principle of respect for persons does not imply its particulars; it is the particulars that we bring together under the broad umbrella of the principle. These specific examples are not mere aids to learning the principle but its essence. The problem is not that most people have not learnt to formulate general principles or a methodology, but rather that they haven't learned to play those countless specific moral games in their everyday lives.

CONCLUSION

One of the consequences of the lack of attention to the prerequisites of education and moral development in particular is the almost exclusive emphasis on moral reasoning and on contrived moral dilemmas at the expense of establishing the virtues, dispositions, and attitudes that have developmental and epistemological primacy. The rationalists have placed imperial reason in the palace while relegating all humble and subservient activities, habits, and virtues to the courtyard. Well, it is time that all those inhabitants of the courtyard be recognized for what they really are – the very strength of the kingdom.

Since language games are embedded in primordial human activities they presuppose a community of human beings who agree not only about definitions and judgments but also in modes of behaviour. Morally significant language games are not created by prophets, philosophers, or sages; they are created by ordinary human beings as they interact among themselves in their numerous and diverse activities. Our moral reasoning is dependent upon these contextual language games and cannot be profitably studied outside them. "The *speaking* of language is part of an activity or of a form of life" – it couldn't be otherwise.

The emphasis on the neglected foundations of education and moral reasoning in particular that is being proposed here requires a change in our method of teaching, especially but not exclusively, the very young. These prerequisites are not established through explicit propositional teaching in institutional settings; they are acquired through early initiation into a particular form of life. There is a necessary social dimension that is missing from rationalist accounts of our whole educational and moral development. The method of teaching that emerges from Wittgenstein's epistemological position is one of apprenticeship, where we initiate the young into our ways of doing things by showing, revealing, and exemplifying desirable behaviour. This method puts severe restrictions both on the educators and the community. Educators must exhibit in their lives all the virtues, habits, and excellences that they intend to impart to the young instead of paying lip service to abstract principles or general methodologies. Society must be a genuine moral and intellectual community where the various human excellences regulate its form of life. Only under such conditions and with such prerequisites in place can we engage safely and profitably in moral reasoning and education.

5

Education as Dialogue

Not the cry, but the rising of the wild duck impels the flock to follow him in flight

Michael Oakeshott

It is quite certain that at no other period in human history has there been so much talk on the need for dialogue; dialogue among members of the family; within communities, regions, and countries; among various churches, religions, and nations. The perceived value of dialogue, however, is usually considered to lie in its instrumental value: it is better for humans to reach an agreement through dialogue rather than through fiat, force, or deception. In order to see how inappropriate and inadequate the instrumental view is we must examine the nature, prerequisites, and principles of dialogue and the social conditions that promote or inhibit it. Furthermore, thinking about education as dialogue will enable us to see more clearly what is intrinsically valuable in education by pointing out the centrality of the moral and intellectual virtues in civilized life and educative teaching. What might not be anticipated is that dialogical teaching is not only the most suitable manner of educating the young, it is also one of the most powerful and effective approaches to teaching; it engages and energizes the students and makes them active participants – not passive receivers.

IN THE BEGINNING WAS DIALOGUE

Whatever the meaning and theological significance of the biblical saying, "In the beginning was the Word [*logos*]," the fact is that, in all things related to human experience, understanding, and development, in the beginning was and is dialogue (*dialogos*). As far as I know, Plato was the first thinker to draw our attention to the dialogical nature of human thinking. In the *Sophist*, the Stranger says: "Well, thinking and discourse are the same thing, except that what we call thinking is, precisely, the inward dialogue carried on by the mind itself without a spoken sound."[1] In other words, thinking is a form of silent conversation with ourselves. In the *Theaetetus*, Socrates repeats the same point and then concludes with his view on the nature of judgment: "when the mind is thinking, it is simply talking to itself, asking questions and answering them, and saying yes and no. When it reaches a decision–which may come slowly or in a sudden rush–when doubt is over and the two voices affirm the same thing, then we call that its 'judgment.' So I should describe thinking as discourse, and judgment as a statement pronounced, not aloud to someone else, but silently to oneself."[2] I think this is one of the most profound ideas about the nature and origin of human thinking and is supported by a great number of modern thinkers. Since we are not born with the ability of carrying on such a discourse within ourselves, the only plausible alternative is that thinking begins with the internalization of the external dialogue as it exists in our social world; if that is the case, it is reasonable to maintain that the quality of our individual thinking must be decisively influenced by the quality of thinking that prevails in our public world.

We can take it as a given today that our thinking, the mind, reason, and the self are neither natural nor divine gifts but develop within the diverse human activities where the various language games are embedded and played. "Logos is the shadow of action," said Democritus a long time ago.[3] It emerges within human actions and reactions and develops or degenerates with them.[4] Reason, then, whatever its biological preconditions, is a distinctly human achievement obtained through dialogue within actual human communities – not an abstract, ethereal, and independent entity outside the context of ordinary life.

The recognition of this point is fundamental to our thinking about education and dialogue, because it frees us from the mythological view of the self and of human reason as fixed, independent, and unchanging creations; redirects our thinking away from the hypothetical private entity called "mind"; and helps us to focus on the real world of human actions, language, intentions, meanings, goals, values, practices, institutions, and customs within which we are all born and develop. It also points to the required social, historical, economic, and political conditions that sustain genuine dialogue and education and those that frustrate or undermine them. It is not a mere historical coincidence that the appearance of the various forms of human understanding and the emergence of dialogue have the same origin and development and coincide with the appearance of democracy in the ancient Greek world; rational dialogue was not present only in the Athenian agora and the everyday activities of the city but also in the dialogues of Plato and all the tragedies and comedies. I do not want to imply that Athenians had achieved pure and untainted dialogue; in their public life dialogue was often flawed or corrupted and the dialogues of Plato are often contrived or fixed. What is important is that perhaps for the first time genuine rational dialogue had a chance to emerge and succeed.

The dialogical nature of human thinking has been emphasized by, among others, Michael Oakeshott, who talks about education as an initiation into a conversation[5] with oneself as well as a "transaction ... between the generations of human beings in which newcomers to the scene are initiated into the world they are to inhabit."[6] In emphasizing the dialogical nature of thinking, Oakeshott refers to the ancient Athenian Antisthenes: "The advantage which Antisthenes claimed to have got from philosophy – 'the advantage of being able to converse with my self' – is the advantage a man may hope to get from education."[7] It is the extent to which we participate in the rich and endless conversation among the generations that determines the character of the internal dialogical thinking within each individual and leads to self understanding and human flourishing. Unlike Oakeshott, however, who talks of education as a conversation among the generations, I prefer to talk of education as dialogue because dialogue, like education, is unquestionably normative and unlike conversation is in every sense caring and engaging and inseparable from the demands of reason. The pursuit of truth and understanding are what give the process of dialogical engagement its direction and purpose and make that process so unique, substantive, and valuable.

The prefix *dia* in *dialogue* means *between* or *through* and thus indicates interpersonal communication, while the word *logos* suggests that the interchange among people is governed by appropriate rules of reasoning; in order for a human contact to be dialogical it must be in accordance with the standards immanent in the various forms of understanding.[8] Dialogue is not an idle chat, discussion, or debate, nor even a conversation. Chatting is usually directionless and purposeless, while in discussion and debate people usually hold relatively fixed positions and try to convince others to change theirs.[9] Dialogue cannot have a predetermined destination, although, as Habermas says: in dialogue there is a "gentle but obstinate, never silent although seldom redeemed claim to reason."[10] The character of conversation, on the other hand, varies according to context, topic, or persons involved: it can be idle, relaxed, passing, playful, or serious, while dialogue has always a serious, challenging, and demanding character. Genuine dialogue is particularly demanding; it requires respect, trust, open-mindedness, and a willingness to listen and risk one's own preconceptions, fixed beliefs, biases, and prejudices in the pursuit of truth. The aim cannot be to win an argument but to advance understanding and human wellbeing. Agreement cannot be imposed but rests on common conviction. Paulo Freire emphasizes in all his writings that, by deepening understanding, dialogical engagement also makes positive changes both in the participants as well as in their world.[11] Hans-Georg Gadamer is in agreement with this portrayal of dialogue, although, like Oakeshott, he uses the word conversation instead. It "is a process of two people understanding each other. Thus it is a characteristic of every true conversation that each opens himself to the other person, truly accepts his point of view as worthy of consideration and gets inside the other ..."[12] He maintains that each person brings their "prejudices or pre-judgments," their "horizon of understanding," to the encounter and the result of this interaction is supposed to be what he calls a "fusion of horizons." Now, all this sounds rather impressive and moving but it is extremely vague. Instead of "prejudices or prejudgments" it would be preferable to talk about beliefs, dispositions, and habits of thought, and instead of "fusion of horizons" it would be more precise to talk about a level of agreement; it is unrealistic to expect two or more people to develop the same horizon of understanding as a result of a dialogical engagement. What is important here, however, is that all these authors who have thought about dialogue seriously agree on the power of mutual respect and understanding to develop the caring, critical, and creative capacities of the participants.

THE PREREQUISITES OF DIALOGUE

Like education and all other complex and refined human attainments, genuine dialogue, which is at the centre of education, has its logical prerequisites in the form of appropriate abilities, dispositions, beliefs, attitudes, emotions, commitments, and virtues. In the previous chapter, I discussed the importance of the distinction between education and its prerequisites, the special ways we acquire prerequisites, and why they constitute essential criteria of rationality. In this chapter, I will sort out the various prerequisites into their appropriate categories in order to demonstrate their vital importance for genuine dialogue and educational development.

Ordinary Certainties

We acquire countless beliefs about the world and about ourselves before we are capable of thinking, doubting, and choosing; and these beliefs are beyond doubt. As we saw earlier, at the level of the hard bedrock of our thought there are the primordial concepts of experience, event, process, state, fact, thing, description, and report; it would be inconceivable to imagine an adult human being in any culture who has not acquired these concepts. Then there are the ordinary certainties in the riverbed of our thinking – such as the beliefs that there is a world with different objects in it, that the Earth was not created yesterday, that the past is unchangeable, and so on – which are universally shared and function as criteria of rationality; those who doubt them or contradict them are not making mistakes, they are behaving irrationally. While there may sometimes be problems in demarcating clearly those universal beliefs from knowledge claims in particular eras or societies (even Wittgenstein, writing in the 1940s, mentioned that the belief that no one has ever been on the moon belongs to the riverbed of our thought!), we can identify a vast number of such beliefs, such as the notion of induction or the existence of the external world, that belong to the realm of the undoubtable foundation of all our thinking; all such beliefs constitute the foundations of our thoughts, judgments, arguments, language, and actions.[13]

There are two important reasons why we ought to distinguish these ordinary certainties from other beliefs. First, because they are part of the riverbed of our thinking and constitute criteria of rationality. Second, very often all kinds of arbitrary doctrines, personal prejudices, dangerous superstitions, or false beliefs are disguised by indoctrinators or propagandists as ordinary certainties belonging to that foundational level of our thinking that does not require justification. Even more insidious are those cases where legitimate ordinary certainties such as "She is a human being" are corrupted by prejudices based on irrelevant facts, such as colour, gender, and ethnicity; the degraded other, then, is treated as an inferior human being. It is one of the great failures of many societies today that they continue to undermine education and genuine dialogue, often in a systematic way, by initiating their young into unwarranted and harmful beliefs that stunt their development as human beings, kill their sense of wonder, inhibit free dialogue, undermine the open society, and ultimately divide the world into warring camps. As we shall see later, doctrinaire religions and ideologies have been among the most repressive and divisive forces in human history and are among the most powerful obstacles to rational dialogue and to an open society. Distinguishing genuine ordinary certainties from doctrines, superstitions, and the like is one of the fundamental tasks of any rational educational theory and policy. In chapter 6 we will have a more extensive discussion on the fundamental difference between the prerequisites of education and the doctrines that are involved in indoctrination.

Rules of Logic

In acquiring language we also acquire a plethora of rules of logic – all of them embedded in ordinary language – such as the rule of non-contradiction, not begging the question, being consistent, and the like; "I am but I am not" does not make any sense in any language, unless the "I" has different referents. It would be impossible to imagine a language without such rules; violating them cannot be considered an option but only a failure to satisfy the fundamental demands of reason. The fact that countless people fail to satisfy the various demands of reason (descriptive relativism) does not mean that such requirements are arbitrary and unfounded, as normative relativism implies; logical fallacies, superstitions, and false or doctrinaire beliefs cannot constitute a challenge to our scientific theories, just as the immoral behaviour of others cannot invalidate our virtues or annul our moral code. The only way we can describe all these human failings is as falling short of the demands of reason. The frequent confusion of descriptive relativism, which is tediously true, with normative relativism, which is not, is deeply regrettable. Although the rules of logic are acquired without the possibility of thinking, doubting, or examining them – as they lie at the foundation of all our thinking – they too can and ought to be identified, clarified, appreciated, and explained later on by all the guardians of excellence within every community and especially by teachers of all subjects at all levels of education.

Moral Virtues

Among the innumerable prerequisites of genuine dialogue and all human flourishing are the ordinary virtues of justice, honesty, and respect for all human beings, cooperation rather than competition, care for others, courage, fair-mindedness, open-mindedness, thoughtfulness, moral sensitivity, and all the other gentle virtues that are summarized by the Greek word *philanthropy*. These virtues are universal in that they are universally recognized human excellences but are not absolute and detached abstractions; they are formed within particular histories, cultures, and shared visions of the good life – they are not specific rules that must be followed but open-ended ideals that must be pursued. As with other ideals they are "ends in view" (to use one of John Dewey's expressions) that cannot be reached but only approximated. We do not expect all people to develop into moral heroes by performing superhuman acts, but we hope that most people will become decent moral agents and will share the essential features of a common vision of the good life. Our moral code has its origin in our biological nature and in our loyalty to our fellow human beings. As a matter of fact, we all have the same basic needs for food, safety, and shelter, and no human being wants to be misled, cheated, enslaved, or tortured. We all recognize that we are expected to be compassionately disposed toward others, and we all consider certain acts as morally exemplary and laudable and others as unspeakable or appalling. In moral education, as in all education, we should not aim at the homogenization of the young – that is what authoritarian and doctrinaire regimes attempt to achieve with their "absolute" doctrines – but at principled pluralism where each person can achieve a measure of individual excellence. Talk about absolutism does not make sense but talk about universalism does; the Protagorean maxim, "Man is the measure of all things" frees us from absolutes but not from universals. "Man" is not the subjective "I" but the universal "we" of all humanity. But the fact is that for each human being there is only the situated human view with our limited abilities, knowledge, experiences, outlooks, and imagination; that view can be broadened and enriched through dialogue. We know that we are totally irrelevant to the cosmos, late arrivals on this planet completely incapable of changing the cosmic order. With dialogue we can expand our horizons and improve our lives. As I will argue later, the only appropriate and positive attitude toward our existence and the existence of the world is one of constant awe and wonder.

It must be clear from the above that virtues are not isolated mechanical habits or skills but manifestations of deep intellectual, moral, emotional, and dispositional commitment to a vision of a worthwhile form of life; our whole being is involved in our virtues. The character of each virtue is not conditional but categorical; there are no calculations that must be performed or hypotheses that must be entertained by the virtuous person – it is only in cases of serious moral dilemmas, lack of relevant knowledge, or strong temptations that we are required to consider alternative courses of action or remind ourselves of our moral duty; the virtuous person performs the moral actions spontaneously. It is this spontaneous categorical imperative in each virtue that allows us to talk about the true character of a person. Virtues are emotively charged enduring traits of character, not fleeting moods, transitory inclinations, useful skills, or momentary preferences. They are manifestations of our authentic commitments to a way of being in the world and to our vision of a life worth living; hence they have motivational or inspirational force that propositional learning usually lacks.

Virtues, like all other human excellences, cannot be organized in a hierarchical order as monistic, deontological, and consequentialist theories suggest. In the domain of morality we must resist the temptation to simplify and unify morality under a single general principle or value. As a matter of fact, all human beings have distinct characters with unique combinations of virtues and weaknesses; one may be more courageous and autonomous than another, but the latter may be more caring and companionate than the former. Our sense of dignity, self-worth, and self-respect is constituted mainly by the virtues that make up our character.

As in all other prerequisites, the development of these virtues requires a genuine moral community where young apprentices can acquire them from authentic exemplars in their everyday lives. The young must begin to live *kata logon* (according to reason) before they are able to live *meta logou* (with or because of reason), as Aristotle aptly put it.[14] The principles of moral behaviour are embedded in the particular actions that are performed *kata logon*; they cannot have a different origin. As Democritus observed, "Many people live according to reason without knowing the moral principle."[15] One needs further special training to formulate the principle. Early habituation in the virtuous way of life is not a matter of choice because there cannot be suitable alternatives to it. The high point in all learning is not learning *that* something is the case (propositional learning), or learning *how* to do something (procedural learning), but learning *to be* a certain kind of person (i.e., just, cooperative, courageous, critical, and the like), that is to say, a person who is committed to the fundamental moral and intellectual excellences that are central to their vision of a life worth living. This development begins with apprenticeship and concrete moral and intellectual models within a civilized human community and not with catechism, preaching, lecturing, ordering, haranguing, intimidating, threatening, punishing, or furious ratiocination – the most common but ineffective alternative practices.

Intellectual Virtues

Equally important for genuine dialogue and human development are the intellectual virtues; like many other human excellences these virtues are not taught separately but are part of all great teaching. Here are Oakeshott's profound comments on the manner in which we acquire the intellectual virtues:

> How does a pupil learn disinterested curiosity, patience, intellectual honesty, exactness, industry, concentration .... doubt ....sensibility to small differences and the ability to recognize intellectual elegance ....the disposition to submit to refutation... and to escape the reproach of fanaticism?.... Learning, then, is acquiring the ability to *feel* and to *think*, and the pupil will never acquire these abilities unless he has learned to listen for them and to recognize them *in the conduct and utterances of others*... (this ability) cannot be learned separately; it is never explicitly learned and it is known *only in practice*; but it may be in everything that is learned...It cannot be learned separately; it can have no

> separate place of its own in a timetable or a curriculum. It cannot be taught overtly by precept because it comprises what is required to animate precept; but it may be taught in everything that is taught. It is implanted unobtrusively in the *manner* in which information is conveyed, in a tone of voice, the gesture which accompanies instruction, in asides and oblique utterances, and by example. For *"teaching by example,"* which is sometimes dismissed as an inferior sort of teaching .... is emancipating the pupil from the half utterances of rules by making him aware of a concrete situation. In imitating the example he acquires not merely a model for the particular occasion, but the disposition to recognize everything as an occasion. It is the habit of listening for an individual intelligence at work in every utterance that may be acquired by *imitating a teacher who has this habit*. And the intellectual virtues may be imparted only by a teacher who cares about them for their own sake and never stoops to the priggishness of mentioning them. Not the cry, but the *rising* of the wild duck impels the flock to follow him in flight.[16]

It would be difficult to imagine a more thoughtful, insightful, or elegant way of explaining and defending the role of examples in establishing the excellences of desirable human development. None of the subtle nuances of moral and intellectual sensitivities can be captured by rules, formulas, or a set of principles. There is, if you like, a powerful tacit dimension to all genuine human actions that is captured by Oakeshott's description. The principles of dialogue that I will refer to later have their foundation in such examples within civilized communities; without them the principles are anemic and hollow slogans. If Oakeshott is correct in emphasizing the primacy of genuine individual human exemplars for all worthwhile human learning, then one can see the fundamental importance of establishing the prerequisites of human development, the severe limitations of all educational technology, and the weaknesses of mere propositional teaching and learning. There cannot be any substitutes for authentic living exemplars of human excellences in a world that is committed to genuine education, meaningful dialogue, and desirable human flourishing. As with all the prerequisites of education and dialogue, the intellectual virtues are acquired, not learned.

Language Games

As we saw earlier, the countless uses of language, such as describing, explaining, complaining, promising, evaluating, reporting, questioning, and so on, are also acquired early in our lives, not learned. This overlooked distinction between *acquisition* and *learning* is actually present in ordinary language: we talk about language acquisition, i.e., acquiring our mother tongue, and about language learning, i.e., learning a foreign language. While we do not acquire language games after critical study and examination, later on the evaluation of their role in different contexts ought to become one of the central tasks of education. Each one of the worthwhile language games has its own inherent public standards that must be adhered to and exemplified unconditionally by educated adults and especially parents and teachers, whose behaviour children imitate. All valuable language games have a normative character: one must report, explain, or promise, according to the standards immanent in each game under appropriate circumstances. These norms are not just skills or know-hows, which one may or may not apply, but intellectual and moral virtues or excellences of an unconditional categorical character; any violation of these inherent standards can be understood only as falling short of the demands of reason. Everyone who describes or promises something ought to be committed to the principles of truth-telling and respect for others; the person who violates these principles is neither a reliable reporter nor a promise-keeper. An equally important educational task is the identification of corrupt or fraudulent language games, such as lying, which undermine genuine dialogue and education. We may choose our lawyers or auto mechanics primarily for their skills and knowledge, which have instrumental value, but we choose our friends or partners for their virtues and lifelong commitments, in other words, for who they truly are.

Since we cannot begin by explicitly teaching language games and their inherent standards – as they are among the presuppositions of all teaching-as-rational-engagement – the only way we can impart them to the very young is through real and concrete everyday examples. One acquires language games just as one acquires intellectual and moral virtues: always within particular social contexts where they are performed with the appropriate feelings, gestures, tone of voice, and manner under appropriate conditions. "I promise," like other language games, is not a mere locution that the young acquire in isolation; it is a complex human act loaded with moral and social significance, absolutely central to the life of any human community. The standards that are embedded in all important language games constitute the foundations of all human thinking and acting with reason and they should be established with the utmost care early in life; later they should be examined and scrutinized within their relevant contexts so that the young can appreciate their fundamental importance for civilized living.

All language games involve relevant beliefs that might sometimes be unfounded and thus lead a person to misdescribing or making unwarranted promises; however, nobody claims that the virtuous person is infallible. Ironically, it is non-virtuous persons who need sophistical skills in order to misrepresent facts and attempt to justify their breaking of promises or misdescribing of events; virtuous persons simply admit their failures and apologize. Those who continue to emphasize the primacy of skills in education are either applying that term very loosely and inappropriately or, more seriously, focusing on educational acquisitions of lesser importance. Equally problematic is the imparting of mere information without adequate attention to the value of the specific language games and their intrinsic standards.

Without moral virtues and intellectual excellences, language games are without their essential foundation and, as a result, rational moral dialogue becomes doubtful, if not impossible. "A person's character is his demon," said Heraclitus, thus stating two important truths. First, that it is a person's character and not some external demon that is the powerful determining factor in their life; and, second, that it is one's character rather than one's skills, abilities, and even knowledge that govern one's life; character is destiny.

THE PRINCIPLES OF DIALOGUE

It is obvious that not every human interaction constitutes an explicit case of dialogue. There are, first, countless forms of effective and appropriate human communication that have an apparent monological form: we report events, tell stories and fables, describe people or things, write poems, express our fears, hopes, loves, desires, and the like. All these monological forms of communication have an essential place in our lives and therefore in teaching. Even these, however, are products of the dialogical nature of our thinking, require the prerequisites I mentioned earlier, and must be performed in a manner that encourages overt dialogue. When they eliminate or inhibit open dialogue they are of lesser value because they might deprive the students of the opportunity to think critically and to interact with others in an open-minded and empathetic way.

On the other hand, there are monological forms of interaction that violate fundamental moral principles and undermine civilized life. If I insult, threaten, deceive, or mock you and you return the insults and the rest, we cannot claim that we are engaged in dialogue. If my general attitude toward others is one of distrust, exploitation, competition, or personal gain, dialogue with them will be seriously undermined.

Genuine dialogue presupposes that all of us are committed to the standards immanent in language games, to the rules of sound reasoning, and to the principles of moral living, especially those of freedom, truth-telling, fairness, and respect for others. Our freedom can be limited only by our obligation to tell the truth and respect others as autonomous and equal agents. Our respect for others means that we care about them and their views, are open to alternative perspectives, and are prepared to modify our views accordingly – always within the demands of reason. These principles are the consciously formulated extensions of the prerequisite virtues that I mentioned earlier and have their origin in these particular virtues; just as we can have no language in the absence of language games and the standards embedded in them, we can have no moral principles without moral virtues.

It is only those persons who exhibit moral virtues in their own lives who can also formulate and interpret the corresponding moral principles. In the beginning are always virtues; principles are derivative and secondary.

In our everyday lives we do not usually make explicit appeals to any logical or moral principles; in all ordinary circumstances we are guided and supported by the moral and intellectual virtues we have acquired through life. Everyday life would be impossible if we had to think about all of our actions and contemplate all alternative choices and their consequences in order to decide what to do in our countless everyday duties and obligations. Only complicated social problems, choices that involve conflicting moral principles, complex problems requiring technical information, courses of action that have unforeseen consequences, or difficult moral choices make it necessary to appeal to moral principles or rules and to try to interpret or apply them. The moral principles without the corresponding virtues would be hollow, anemic, and ineffectual to a non-moral agent. It is often argued that our ordinary, garden-variety virtues do not help us to resolve complex ethical problems and dilemmas, that for such problems we need general moral principles. The truth is that in discussing such difficult problems the participants may need new information, or they may disagree on which virtue or principle should be overriding, or, as is often the case, they do not have the prerequisites to engage in genuine dialogue. In all instances of problem-solving it is virtues that do the real work, while principles may often degenerate into high-sounding but empty partisan slogans. It is true that our virtues may not enable us to solve ultimate moral dilemmas, but there is nothing else that can do that either. To the extent that there are ultimate moral dilemmas, they point to the dramatic character of human life, and nothing can help us – that is what ultimate dilemmas are. In fact, it is only the virtuous person with a deep commitment to a moral way of life who can truly experience moral dilemmas; such dilemmas are not detached intellectual problems like logical paradoxes, they are deep personal disquietudes that suggest the limits of human reason. It is a common belief that we can resolve all moral dilemmas rationally; I consider that belief to be unwarranted. A compassionate society should recognize both the demands and limits of reason and allow people to make their difficult existential decisions in freedom and responsibility. Only doctrinaire individuals will have answers for all moral dilemmas, but such positions are arbitrary, just like their underlying doctrines. The so-called "moral dilemmas approach" to moral education can only be a way of dealing with situations where there are conflicting moral principles that can be resolved by determining which principles are justifiably overriding in particular cases. Although these can be useful exercises when we deal with actual conflicts in children's lives, they are by no means the only or the most important aspect of moral education. People who are not committed to a virtuous life cannot take part meaningfully and profitably in solving difficult moral problems.

THE CHARACTER OF GENUINE DIALOGUE

From what has been said so far it is apparent that dialogue is the highest form of human communication; it presupposes and develops further all the quiet virtues that underlie the foundations of civilized life. The primary purpose of dialogue is not to convince or influence others but to understand their perspectives, concerns, values, emotional states, assumptions, and goals. "A conversation," says Oakeshott:

> does not need a chairman, it has no predetermined course, we do not ask what it is "for," and we do not judge its excellence by its conclusion; it has no conclusion, but it is always put by for another day. Its integration is not superimposed but springs from the quality of the voices which speak, and its value lies in the relics it leaves behind in the minds of those who participate.[17]

Like genuine scientific inquiry, dialogue does not have prearranged objectives; its character is determined by the standards inherent in the language games and the intellectual and moral virtues that are also enshrined in the character of the participants. For that reason dialogue does not need masters, directors, coaches, leaders, or supervisors who want to impose their views, values, ideas, and ways of life on others. On the contrary, dialogue and a civilization that is based on it are free and open and cannot survive within authoritarian hierarchies, arbitrary doctrines, or patronizing and priggish monologues. Those who participate in genuine dialogue do not try to protect themselves behind their favourite nonnegotiable doctrines, prejudices, preferences, or slogans; they do not give orders and do not behave like prophets, lawmakers, or revolutionaries. On the contrary, they express their opinions, fears, hopes, and doubts and listen to their interlocutors with patience, interest, sensitivity, respect, care, and understanding. It is not that they do not have disagreements, but their disagreements are opportunities for more self-examination and understanding rather than occasions for self-promotion, triumphant boasting, or offending others.

The ideal case of dialogue is where two friends confide in each other in a trusting way without fear of being ridiculed, offended, or let down. In a friendly dialogue we transcend personal ambitions and desires and turn our attention to the needs of our friend and the demands of the problem we are discussing. Without such transcendence – which has its foundations in our moral character, our vision of the good life, our knowledge of the subject, and the wisdom we have acquired about the human condition – there cannot be constructive dialogue. However, even the most ideal dialogical engagement does not mean that we can completely identify with our friend; that would mean a fusion of our two selves – which is impossible. Genuine dialogue enables us to become aware of the beliefs, values, and commitments that constitute our self-identity and, at the same time, achieve a sympathetic understanding of the other. Neither of these achievements, however, is final, because dialogue is open-ended, dynamic, and constantly evolving, as are we the participants.

True dialogue has its own ritual, its rhythmic flow and harmony, without loud, strident, or harsh sounds. The give-and-take is complimentary, inclusive, appreciative, and supportive; it is not negative or antagonistic. There is an aesthetic dimension to dialogue that is violated by excess, authoritarianism, self-interest, and self-promotion. It is in dialogue, more than in any other human activity, that we can recognize the subtle interweaving of the moral and the aesthetic features into intricate human excellences. Like other virtues, these excellences are qualities of character that suggest profound personal development with appropriate behavioural manifestations. Qualities such as gracefulness, politeness, civility, compassion, consideration, refinement, thoughtfulness, sensitivity, gentleness, kindness, patience, and other such gentle virtues are stable and lasting inner dispositions rather than temporary or passing moods, feelings, or preferences. It is on the basis of such traits that we choose our friends and partners and engage in genuine dialogue with others; for moral as well as aesthetic reasons we disapprove of people who are uncouth, ill-mannered, unpleasant, rude, crude, gross, offensive, boorish, uncivil, and uncultured.

It is odd that these desirable qualities of mind and character usually do not appear among the virtues studied by moral philosophers, social scientists, or theologians; and yet they are vital to human relationships and essential to genuine dialogue. Perhaps the reason for this omission is the erroneous belief that these excellences are not central to a moral code or that they are primarily aesthetic qualities. The truth is that these excellences are hybrid virtues in which the moral and the aesthetic are integrated. Clear instances of such hybrid virtues can be found in examples such as "she (or he) is a *beautiful* person," while the absence of these virtues makes them and their way of life "ugly" – we use these two terms that normally belong in the aesthetic domain in order to describe the moral character of persons or a morally repulsive way of life. Plato's view that the beautiful is part of the good seems appropriate here, if we understand the "good" to be simply our vision of the good life; the vision of a life worth living of any mature moral agent cannot be deprived of aesthetic qualities such as harmony, symmetry, and balance. This idea of harmony pervades all ancient Greek thought: it is present in Plato's view of justice as harmony among the various excellences of the soul as well as among the various classes of citizens in the *Republic*; it is also central to Aristotle's definition of virtue (in the *Nichomachean Ethics*) as a mean between two extremes. According to Heraclitus even "the sun will not transgress his measures; otherwise the Furies, ministers of Justice, will find him out."[18] The Furies in Greek mythology are the upholders of natural and moral order in the world. It is apparent that vulgar, crude, gross, coarse, and disgusting behaviour violates both moral and aesthetic criteria. The above hybrid virtues are fundamental to all genuine dialogue and to any form of civilized life.

One might argue that the above analysis is utopian because it presents dialogue in its ideal form. But while the point about being the presentation of an ideal is correct, the claim about it being utopian is not. It is true that dialogue is always to some extent imperfect, flawed, inadequate, or disappointing; that is why I have been speaking of genuine dialogue. The present analysis, to the extent that it is successful, gives us the necessary criteria on the basis of which we can judge the extent to which an individual, institution, or society supports or undermines dialogue. Our world would be extremely impoverished without ideals; they are indispensable, because they show us the desired course for our thoughts, choices, and actions.

THE APPROPRIATE CONDITIONS OF DIALOGUE AND EDUCATION

Although empirical research can provide us with valuable information regarding the social and psychological conditions that are conducive or detrimental to dialogue, no amount of sociological, historical, or ethnological research can establish the criteria of genuine dialogue; true dialogue is a human achievement, not a given in human nature, and the task of demarcating its criteria is a philosophical one. Those who speak about different "forms" of dialogue in different cultures or groups are like those who confuse the code of conduct of a particular community with its moral code; the Nazis and all Mafia-type groups have their own codes of conduct, which are in large part immoral. *Dialogue* is not like the concept of *game*, where we have multiple criteria for the application of the term and where the criteria vary according to the form of the game. There cannot be one ideal, superior, genuine game – such as soccer or hockey – as opposed to other defective or inferior games; they are all legitimate games. But that is precisely what we say about dialogue: there are better and worse cases (not forms) of dialogue depending on the extent to which they satisfy its criteria. The consequences of abandoning the criteria of dialogue amount to undermining civilized life. It is, of course, always advisable to re-examine these criteria when confronted with objections; being open to reasonable challenges is one of the criteria of dialogue. As we abandon our tribal rules and practices and embrace universal moral principles we enhance dialogue, promote education, and protect our society and our world.

Dialogue cannot take place in a social vacuum; the cultural, political, and economic conditions of society influence decisively the quality of dialogue and education within it. The institutionalization of important human activities in a society is a mixed blessing; perhaps it is most damaging in the area of education, where it is assumed that the school is its primary agent and all other institutions have no educational responsibilities. When we consider the fundamental importance of the prerequisites of education, for which the school plays an important but secondary role, we can see the seriousness of the problem; the family's central role in securing the prerequisites of human flourishing has not been appreciated, studied and supported adequately. A society educates its citizens not exclusively through its schools, but also through its laws, customs and traditions, its various institutions, social structures and practices, its intellectual, aesthetic and political achievements and all its everyday cultural activities. It is a dangerous mistake to think that education and its prerequisites start or end in the public schools; the whole society cultivates the character, mind, sensibilities, and tastes of its citizens, or it neglects and corrupts them. In an educating society all institutions and all citizens have important educational responsibilities. There are certain societal conditions that promote education and dialogue and other conditions that frustrate and undermine them. Children who live in abject poverty and those who have been neglected, mistreated, or traumatized are unlikely to have acquired the prerequisites to engage in rational dialogue; on the contrary, they usually have acquired habits, attitudes, and beliefs that undermine their educational development and their disposition for genuine rational dialogue. Likewise, authoritarian, rigid, and biased teachers and arbitrary and inflexible bureaucratic schools frustrate dialogue and undermine education.

There are several political and economic conditions that facilitate dialogue and others that are opposed to it. Inequality, poverty, exploitation, greed, fear and uncertainty, authoritarianism, and the use of force are wholly inimical to dialogue. Relentless competition among individuals and nations is one of its greatest enemies. Violence is usually the result of lack of equality and is caused mainly by the exploitation of the weak. "Equality does not cause wars," said Solon long ago – if, of course, the principle of equality is accepted unconditionally as fundamental by all people. The economic and political imperialism whose goal is the subjugation and exploitation of people violates the criteria of dialogue and is incompatible with the demands of civilized society.

Dialogue is also incompatible with doctrinaire and theocratic societies and institutions. The world is divided today, as it has been for centuries, by arbitrary doctrines that "legitimize" authoritarian and inhumane regimes. There cannot exist genuine dialogue among institutions that are founded on "infallible," absolute, and non-negotiable doctrines. Likewise, aggressive political negotiations, antagonistic bargaining, and disputes do not constitute dialogue.

DIALOGUE AND EDUCATION

It is no mere coincidence that the prerequisites of dialogue are also the prerequisites of education and that the principles of dialogue are at the foundation of all genuine educational curricula. The best way to view education is to consider it as a form of free, open, informed dialogue among all members of society, and the educational system as a deliberate genuine dialogue between the younger and older generations on all matters having to do with the human condition. Dialogue, like education, has a horizontal dimension embracing all the worthwhile voices of humankind, past and present. It also has a vertical dimension, where it explores "the why of things," as Richard Peters put it, i.e., the reasons for our choices, actions, policies, and laws and the causes of all natural phenomena. Dialogue begins early in the immediate, familial environment and continues with the voices of the past and present and the geographically distant. One does not carry on a dialogue only with the members of one's family and friends but also with the authors of the books one reads or the recorded voices one hears, although, for obvious reasons, the dialogical nature of this kind of interaction is limited.

Free dialogue energizes, motivates, cultivates, and reinforces our character and our mind, whereas monologue and imposition frustrate and inhibit critical and creative thinking. Not only should dialogue be at the centre of all education, it might well be the most effective method of teaching the young. When educational institutions function as centres of dialogue they become genuine human communities of openness, respect, trust, and cooperation that motivate the students and promote long-lasting and transformative learning. It is that kind of environment that creates the special ethos of a first-rate school and makes it a special place where the students are alert, attentive, content, and motivated.

The dialogical view of human thinking frees us also from the view of the mind as an information processing machine or as a room where we store information in order to retrieve it later; these views of the human mind have had, probably, the most harmful consequences for educational theory and practice; they overlook or de-emphasize the worthwhile attainments of humanity that constitute the substance of education and misdirect us to the imaginary "processes" of an invented entity called *the mind*.

Thinking of education as dialogue points to another way of emphasizing the non-instrumental nature of genuine education and distinguishes it from training. Just as genuine dialogue cultivates and enriches a person's mind and character, successful education results in the transformation of the person; it is this important criterion that R.S. Peters emphasized when he said that educated persons are not those who have arrived at their destination but those who are travelling with a different view. The educated person, just like the genuine participant in dialogue, abides by the standards that are embedded in language games in their varied contexts. As I argued earlier, the demands of all language games and intellectual and moral virtues are not conditional but categorical and definitive of a person's character and way of life. Education is the development of persons, not the training of soldiers, lawyers, or computer technicians. The character of all training depends on a job, task, or role for which the individual is being prepared. Education, on the other hand, is not a preparation for anything; its aims are inherent within itself. Unlike training and like dialogue, education has no aims; the appropriate questions to ask about education and dialogue are what they mean, what values they summarize, what is their place within a civilized society – not what they aim at or for. Being educated is a way of being in the world and a way of living one's life. Looking at education through the criteria of dialogue enables us to see more clearly the centrality of character development and the importance of the moral and intellectual virtues and principles that ought to govern all human activities.

What both dialogue and education emphasize is the absolute centrality of the intellectual and moral virtues for individual and collective wellbeing. Nothing else will improve our educational institutions and the character of our civilization as much as our efforts to cultivate genuine rational dialogue within our schools as well as within our world; it is through dialogical teaching that we can put children on their lifelong path to self-education. "Education as Dialogue," as I have attempted to interpret and defend it above, is, in my view, the most appropriate antidote to our divided, confused, rudderless, and competitive world.

6

Forms of Miseducation

Although most educators would agree that indoctrination is the most pernicious enemy of both education and dialogue, since it violates the knowledge criterion of education and distorts the value criterion, there are still those who continue to support the teaching of doctrines in the name of education. The proponents of that view employ several arguments – all of which, in my view, are philosophically wanting. Perhaps the most common strategy of the advocates of indoctrination is to so relax the criteria of education as to render it indistinguishable from that hazy, all-embracing and confusing term, *socialization*. First, then, we must examine the concept of socialization in order to determine whether one can justifiably and fruitfully define education as socialization.

SOCIALIZATION

Unlike *education*, *socialization* has no proper home in ordinary language; it entered educational discourse from the social sciences and in the process has changed its meaning. For social scientists socialization is a descriptive term that refers to certain social processes, whereas in educational writings it is used as a normative word that appears usually in statements about "the aims of education."

An impatient critic of the claim that education is the socialization of the young might be inclined to declare that once again the language of education has gone on holiday and refuse to deal with the claim and the problems it creates. It might be prudent, however, to discuss socialization further in the hope that some important truths about education, socialization, and indoctrination may be highlighted more prominently.

Social scientists use the term *socialization* to refer to the diverse and complex processes by which young children, born with considerable potential for different types of behaviour, come to adopt the specific language, customs, beliefs, standards, and values of their society.[1] One cannot be overimpressed by the extent to which particular societies and social groups determine the way the young come to think, feel, relate to people, evaluate things, and express themselves. Social scientists have divided these agencies of socialization into primary groups (family, children's playgroups, and close-knit neighbourhoods) and secondary groups (large corporations, universities, and the army). The primary groups, "the nursery of human nature,"[2] as Charles H. Cooley called them, have greater molding power on the young than the secondary groups because of the face-to-face interaction, sentiments of loyalty, emotional involvement, and close cooperation among their members. It is obvious that all formal or informal social and educational influences on the young are considered by social scientists as aspects of this all-inclusive process of socialization. Schools are usually classified as secondary groups along with churches, clubs, and other institutions.

Humans are social animals who owe their humanity to their community; as we shall see in the final chapter, human nature is neither there in the newborn child nor does it unfold mechanically in accordance with its own laws. Its development depends, in a decisive way, on the quality of human interactions experienced by the child: human nature "comes into existence through fellowship and decays in isolation."[3] The various socializing agencies encourage, liberate, and channel or restrict, constrain, and suppress the undifferentiated human potential in each child and thus determine to a large extent a person's moral, intellectual, and emotional development. According to George Herbert Mead:

> The self is something which has a development; it is not initially there, at birth, but arises in the process of social experience and activity, that is, develops in the given individual as a result of his relations to that process as a whole and to other individuals within that process.[4]

Any person who is interested in building a theory of education or in making educational policy must examine these and other claims made by social scientists. Without valid information on the effects of various socializing agencies on the young, educational policymakers cannot determine the boundary conditions of educational policy in a particular society or the extent to which basic prerequisites of education for all young people in that society have been established adequately and suitably. When such information is lacking, educational policy tends to be utopian, setting unrealistic goals and expectations for both students and teachers.

The Slogan

Serious trouble starts when this perfectly legitimate talk about socialization in the social sciences drops its descriptive garment and then reappears as an explicit prescription among educational policymakers. Its most common form, in this new role, is the pseudoscientific version of the functionalist argument. The original and most sophisticated architect of this argument is Emile Durkheim. Usually among his followers are the educational policymakers and administrators who work in ministries of education or serve in the educational systems of most nations.

According to Durkheim and his followers there are no values specific or central to education. "Education is *only the means* by which society prepares, within the children, the essential conditions of its very existence ... Education consists of a methodical socialization of the young."[5] Durkheim's definition of education makes it clear that in his view there are no specific criteria of education. The principles that determine the objectives and the content of education are to be found in the particular society and the special group to which the citizens belong:

> Education is the influence exercised by adult generations on those that are not yet ready for social life. Its object is to arouse and to develop in the child a certain number of physical, intellectual and moral states which are demanded of him by both the political society as a whole and the special milieu for which he is specifically destined.[6]

Durkheim's conception of education was greatly influenced by his negative view of human nature and by his total preoccupation with the survival of society – in these two respects his views are consistent with the views of most conservative political and educational theorists since Plato. They would all disagree with John Dewey that education "has no end beyond itself," that "it is its own end,"[7] or they would agree with Plato that education, in its normative sense that I discussed earlier, could be possible only for a select few.

Durkheim sees only the antisocial, egoistic side of individuals who are not inclined to submit to political authority spontaneously, dedicate themselves to society, or sacrifice themselves for their fellow citizens. All citizens, therefore, must be methodically socialized, that is, taught, indoctrinated, conditioned, trained, or constrained to acquire those attributes that will guarantee the survival of their society.

Durkheim's functionalist argument is as follows. There are some theorists who:

> assume that there is an ideal, perfect education, which applies to all men indiscriminately; and it is this education, universal and unique, that the theorist tries to define. But first, if history is taken into consideration, one finds in it nothing to confirm such a hypothesis. Education has varied infinitely in time and place. In the cities of Greece and Rome education trained the individual to subordinate himself blindly to the collectivity ... Today, it tries to make of an individual an autonomous personality. In Athens, they sought to form cultivated souls, informed, subtle, full of measure and harmony, capable of enjoying beauty and the joys of pure speculation; in Rome, they wanted above all

> for children to become men of action ... In the Middle Ages, education was above all Christian; in the Renaissance, it assumes a more lay and literary character.[8]

It is clear that Durkheim is talking here not about the meaning of education but the diverse functions of schools in various societies. But the historical question of what various societies have tried to achieve through their schools is surely not the same as the important questions that educational theorists try to answer: "What does it mean to educate a person?" or "Who is the educated person?" It would be naive to misconstrue these philosophical questions as if they were empirical questions about the functions of schools.

There is no a priori reason, of course, why public schools in different societies, including our own, should be educational institutions; they could function as centres of indoctrination, training, and socialization, like the schools of Sparta and many other stifling, closed societies. What is of great importance is that if public schools are to function as educational institutions, then, as we saw earlier, we have certain legitimate expectations of them: that they introduce the young into some worthwhile knowledge and understanding, rather than indoctrinate, exploit, or merely train them as soldiers or professionals. If public schools abandon their educational responsibilities, then those who value education must think of other ways of educating their young – perhaps that is one of the reasons some parents today take their children out of the public schools and send them to private schools: to get a better education.

After having taken us on his grand tour of the functions of schooling in diverse societies, Durkheim asks a rhetorical question and then proceeds to buttress up his functionalist argument with a series of pseudo-dilemmas.

> Can it be said, then, that the fact is not the ideal; that if education has varied, it is because men have mistaken what it should be? But if Roman education had been infused with an individualism comparable to ours, the Roman city would not have been able to maintain itself; Latin civilization would not

> have developed, nor, furthermore, our modern civilization, which is in part descended from it. The Christian societies of the Middle Ages would not have been able to survive if they had given to free inquiry the place that we give it today. There are, then, ineluctable necessities which it is impossible to disregard. Of what use is it to imagine a kind of education that would be fatal for the society that put it into practice?[9]

It is necessary to examine the strength and legitimacy of this argument because it is used often by all those who blindly or deliberately support infamous social orders, institutions, or policies. The first problem is one of ambiguity: is Durkheim talking about the survival of the individuals who constitute those societies or is he referring to the variety of institutions, customs, and values of these societies? If he means the former, then he is making outlandish empirical claims that cannot be supported by evidence and sound arguments. If, on the other hand, he is talking about the survival of particular institutions, values, and the like, then his argument is mere tautology. "It is tediously a necessary condition of the survival of a group-with-certain-values that the group should retain those values."[10] It is true, then, that "the Christian societies of the Middle Ages would not have been able to survive" as Christian societies of the Middle Ages "if they had given to free inquiry the place that we give it today." The problem is that these "necessities" that Durkheim talks about are "ineluctable" only because they are redundant rhetorical tautologies.

The only instances where functionalist arguments are appropriate are cases in which certain institutions, values, beliefs, customs, and the like are so inextricably connected with the whole fabric of society that any sudden or violent change, suspension, or suppression of them could have much greater consequences for the people than might be expected. "Such propositions, if established, would of course be of first importance in deciding what to do; but they cannot take over the work of deciding what to do."[11] This is probably among the soundest of arguments for supporting piecemeal evolution within societies.

The second problem with Durkheim's claims stems from the vagueness of the word *survival*. Survival, simpliciter, is never the goal of individuals, societies, institutions, policies, or programs; it is always a certain quality of survival that people want to attain. For the present discussion, then, the real issue is the nature of values that are specific to education and the quality of life they imply for the individual and for society. Vague talk about socialization and survival avoids that important issue and creates, instead, one of the most deceptive educational slogans – education as socialization – most often used by those who want to introduce some form of indoctrination into educational institutions.

By reducing education only to a means, Durkheim strips it of its knowledge and value criteria. It is now a chameleonic term more or less synonymous with schooling and has to adopt the character of the political and economic order it is designed to perpetuate. That conception of education, however, can no longer provide any direction to our educational thinking, research, planning, or practice; in the hands of Durkheim and his followers it has become a dull and primitive instrument.

There are several reasons social scientists omit the differentia of education (i.e., worthwhile knowledge and understanding) from their definition and talk about it only in terms of its genus (i.e., socialization or acculturation). Social psychologists, for example, want to draw attention to the social nature of the self and thus to emphasize a necessary condition for human development. Sociologists and anthropologists talk of education as socialization to stress the fact that by and large societies try to ensure the survival of the dominant beliefs, values, and customs in their cultures through a formal initiation of the young.

The question is why do some educational theorists and policymakers adopt the language of the social scientists and talk about education as socialization. If we examine the beliefs and values that are transmitted to the young through the "process of socialization" we shall discover that not all of them are educationally significant or legitimate: some of them could be described as necessary prerequisites of education (acquiring the language, habits, beliefs, virtues, and attitudes that I discussed earlier); some may be described as having educational value (learning to respect evidence and to construct valid arguments within the various forms of knowledge and understanding); others may be described as non-educational (learning to swim, dress, or hold a fork properly); and still others may be classified as miseducational (learning false beliefs, doctrines, prejudices, and the like). Some of those aspects of socialization, such as acquiring the prerequisites, are not optional but a necessary condition for a child's development as a human being. The most effective kind of socialization is informal and does not require unnecessary institutionalization; it is in the interest of the young to acquire the useful skills, habits, beliefs, and values that are the prerequisites of education.

One can only speculate as to the reasons that entice educators and others to use the socialization slogan when they want to talk about the nature of education and the aims of educational institutions. The reasons seem to range from the understandable to the deceptive and dangerous.

One interpretation of this slogan is that it is a reaction against certain romantic views of education that consider it as the spontaneous unfolding of human potentialities or merely as the facilitation of the natural growth and development of the child. The function of this slogan is to disapprove of such romantic views of human nature and to remind us that no newborn child can develop into a mature person without the humanizing influence of the social group. It is also to remind the proponents of such utopian educational doctrines that the staples of education – beliefs, values, dispositions, skills, knowledge, and tastes – are public achievements and not natural givens or unfoldings within each individual person.

More often, however, the claim that education is the socialization of the young is politically motivated and is used by the guardians of the sociopolitical status quo in order to preserve their policies, programs, and practices and to ward off unwanted criticism and evaluation of them. This attitude, which is characteristic of all closed societies, is a clear indication that in the educational system of such societies there exist at least some of the conditions and ingredients of indoctrination, such as authoritarian structures, fear of open dialogue, questionable beliefs and doctrines, blind commitment to beliefs, institutions and policies, widespread misology, and an assortment of educationally illegitimate methods. It is this ambiguity in the use of the term *socialization* that makes the socialization slogan one of the most deceptive and dangerous in education.

Proponents of indoctrination usually feel uncomfortable with a clear demarcation between education and socialization. They prefer to ignore the specific normative sense of education, which implies knowledge and understanding and the intersubjective demands of reason, and to dwell instead on the broadest use of *education*, which is synonymous with socialization or acculturation. Within that vague and amorphous sense of education the distinction between education and indoctrination is obliterated.

THE NATURE OF INDOCTRINATION

Although few concepts have been subjected to such extended and systematic philosophical scrutiny as has *indoctrination*, there are still serious disagreements with regard to its exact nature. Consequently, we lack an agreed upon criterion for our educational judgments, deliberations, and decisions, and our educational policy remains unclear with respect to indoctrination. This is certainly a serious deficiency, since, whatever our criterion of it, we all seem to agree, outside the world of various extreme religious fundamentalisms, that indoctrination is one of the most serious and widespread forms of miseducation.

My view concerning the causes of these disagreements is that they are due largely to carelessness or to the programmatic intentions of some writers on indoctrination and not to the hopeless vagueness or the inherent intractability of the concept. Prominent among such writers are the proponents of religious indoctrination who have been reluctant to accept the view that the primary locus of indoctrination is fundamentalist religion. They have maintained, instead, that doctrines are equally common in science and other areas and that the criterion of whether a person is indoctrinating is not the doctrinal beliefs that are being inculcated but the miseducative methods or intentions of the teacher. In this chapter I shall argue that indoctrination is but one form of miseducation that must be distinguished from other forms, such as propaganda; that it can be explicated only in terms of doctrinal beliefs that are religious or quasi-religious; that there cannot be such doctrines in science[12]; and that the questionable methods used by indoctrinators together with their intentions are parasitic on the doctrines that are being inculcated.

The Context of Indoctrination

When philosophers say that we ought to examine the various uses of words in their actual contexts they do not mean that we must consult our dictionaries and enumerate all the various uses of the word we want to clarify.[13] Although such practices may be useful for other purposes they cannot settle any philosophical questions; indeed they very often bring forth linguistic skeletons from bygone ages that add further confusions to the subject under examination. What philosophers have in mind is the study and explication of current linguistic usage.[14] If words are, among other things, necessary tools then we must examine our tools in order to find out what actual work they perform in our language today and for what purposes. It might be interesting to explore the reasons why in the Middle Ages the word indoctrination was used interchangeably with education or teaching, but that inquiry would not sufficiently clarify our concepts of indoctrination, education, or teaching today.

Our concern about indoctrination stems, first, from our commitment to education and dialogue and the specific epistemological and value constraints that these terms impose on various activities, programs, and institutions. In other words, education implies worthwhile knowledge and understanding and therefore rules out superstitions, prejudices, doctrines, false beliefs, and the like. Our second reason is that, while indoctrinated people are unwilling or incapable of subjecting their doctrinal beliefs to rational scrutiny, many of them, nonetheless, want their doctrines to function as regulative principles of the way of life of the whole society. It is obvious, then, that indoctrination presents a very serious political problem to the modern world.

The paradigm cases of indoctrination are to be found in fundamentalist religions, and all uses of *indoctrination* suggest that it has to do with the transmission or inculcation of specific doctrinal beliefs. Ayatollahs, popes, patriarchs, and televangelists are not interested in indoctrination in general – because there is no such thing – but in the inculcation of specific doctrines that are foundational to their respective ways of life. The prepositional modifiers *into* and *with*, which accompany ordinary uses of the verb *to indoctrinate*, suggest that the doctrinal beliefs must be specific; thus one indoctrinates the young *into* the doctrines of a particular church or *with* the doctrines of a specific ideology. In this respect "indoctrinating *into* or *with*" behaves like "training *in*": in both cases the prepositions limit the scope of their respective activities and specify their objectives.

Successful indoctrination results in the acceptance of doctrinal beliefs and commitment to them, whereas successful educational engagements aim at some worthwhile understanding and autonomous critical thinking. If students, after careful consideration, reject the doctrines they have been taught, the indoctrinator has failed. On the other hand, if a student rejects with convincing arguments the claims made in a school textbook, we do not say that the teacher has failed as an educator; in fact, if the student's questioning is based on clear understanding and reasonable arguments, we might even conclude that this episode was a paradigm case of educative teaching and learning.

It is not uncommon for people to confuse the indoctrinated person with a doctrinaire, rigid, or inflexible individual; although there is considerable overlap between them, these concepts are distinct. The problem with doctrinaire persons has to do mainly with their character, temperament, or narrow outlook, whereas the problem with indoctrinated persons has to do primarily with the nature of the doctrinal beliefs to which they are committed; that is why indoctrinated people can very often free themselves from doctrines when they get an education, whereas doctrinaire persons usually do not change. The educational problems that these two cases present are notably different; in the first case we have to address primarily the psychological problems of the person who feels uncomfortable with doubt and uncertainty, whereas in the second case we must deal mainly with the epistemological status of certain doctrinal beliefs that are not within the realm of human reason; the task in this chapter is to deal with the latter problem.

Indoctrination and Intentions

Most existing discussions of indoctrination fail to provide a clear demarcation of the concept either because they fail to identify the correct criterion of indoctrination, or, if they do, they fail to describe it properly. In the first category are those who take intention or method to be the criterion, while in the second are those who consider content to be the criterion of indoctrination.

Of the first two proposed criteria, intention is the stronger candidate as it is on the basis of people's intentions that we characterize their actions and not primarily on the basis of some behavioural descriptions of what they do or on the results of their actions. In most cases where we talk of teachers indoctrinating their students we refer to their intentions to manipulate the young so that they suspend their critical thinking and become committed to certain doctrines at the expense of any other legitimate alternative beliefs. The intention, however, is always parasitic on the doctrines that are being inculcated. In the absence of doctrines one cannot have any intention to indoctrinate, although one can still miseducate in countless ways. Just as *teaching* implies a triadic relationship between the teacher, the student, and what is being taught, *indoctrination* implies a similar relationship between the indoctrinator, the learner, and the doctrines in question. In fact this relationship is stricter in the case of indoctrinating than it is in teaching. In ordinary language we talk about the "self-taught" person but not about the "self-indoctrinated" one. The reason is that in the first case the teacher and the pupil are one and the same person, while in the case of indoctrination an external agent is required. The reason for this discrepancy has to do with the nature of doctrines. Self-taught persons are those who, after having acquired the prerequisites of rational thinking and inquiry, have discovered by themselves certain truths or new ways of doing things, have developed certain skills or cultivated better tastes, have improved their methods of doing things or discovered new ones. All these things they acquired by trial and error, by following certain rules, by avoiding pitfalls and blind alleys, by correcting their errors, and by applying new techniques. For all these achievements the self-taught persons make use of public criteria, rules, procedures, and tests; in other words, self-taught persons must come up to certain public standards. Doctrines, superstitions, biases, and false beliers are not the sort of things that one can be said to have discovered or attained because there are no public, intersubjective, non-sectarian standards they can satisfy. What can it possibly mean to talk of the discovery of the doctrine of the infallibility of the pope, the triadic nature of the Christian deity, or the filioque? We do not talk about discovering gibberish, even when it appears to be new, complex, and sophisticated; we can only fabricate or invent it.

A second reason for rejecting the intention criterion of indoctrination as sufficient in itself is that it is of little use for educational planning. A philosophical examination of indoctrination should offer the educational community a clearly demarcated concept that can be used in making important educational decisions regarding the content and methods that are appropriate for educational institutions. A view of indoctrination that is based exclusively on the intention of the teacher cannot exclude even the most pernicious doctrines from the curriculum. While no educational policymaker can control the intentions of teachers, every responsible educational planner can and must purify the educational curriculum by eliminating doctrinal and other unfounded beliefs from it.

My third objection to the intention criterion is that it overlooks the unintended consequences of human actions. Just as we can insult, embarrass, infuriate, or intimidate other people without having the slightest intention of doing so, we may indoctrinate or otherwise miseducate them unintentionally. Surely, educational (and social) planning that disregards the unintended consequences of our actions, programs, policies, and institutional arrangements must be considered seriously lacking, if not dangerous. It concentrates exclusively on the good intentions of teachers and overlooks the actual consequences of our interventions in the lives of the young.

Finally, proponents of the intention criterion of indoctrination consistently overlook the fact that, like education, indoctrination has not only an intentional sense but also a success or achievement sense, when it refers to the indoctrinated person. When we want to discover whether the students have been indoctrinated the intentions of the teacher are simply irrelevant. The only criterion that is relevant here is the novices' commitment to certain doctrines; if there is no commitment to specific doctrines we cannot talk about successful indoctrination.

Indoctrination and Methods

The last argument against the intention criterion applies as well to the method criterion of indoctrination. The methods used by indoctrinators are irrelevant when we want to ascertain whether a person has been indoctrinated. Commitment to certain doctrinal beliefs – and only this – is the necessary and sufficient criterion for the students' to have been indoctrinated. In order for method to be an adequate criterion of indoctrination there must be methods peculiar to it. It is obvious, however, that there are no such methods. The indoctrinators, because they are inculcating doctrines, must resort to some educationally questionable methods such as failing to provide relevant evidence and arguments or suppressing them, misusing their authority, and the like. These and other such methods, however, can be used for all sorts of educationally illegitimate purposes, not just indoctrination. An account of indoctrination in terms of method alone makes it synonymous with miseducation and thus renders it an ineffective, blunt tool – there are countless ways to miseducate. The issue is not whether indoctrination is a form of miseducation but what sort of miseducation it is and how it differs from other sorts of miseducation, such as propaganda.

The proponents of the method criterion invariably fail to distinguish between indoctrination and propaganda. Although propagandists often resort to indoctrination it is not necessary for them to do so. In typical cases the indoctrinators believe that their doctrines are true or give meaning to life, or that they will bring about peace and justice on Earth. In trying to inculcate their doctrines the indoctrinators offer some reasons and some evidence, but their reasons and evidence are based primarily on parochial, subjective, or arbitrary grounds. However, indoctrinators are not necessarily like the pernicious propagandists who conceal or misrepresent facts, appeal to emotions, resort to threats, or hide their real motives in order to influence the beliefs and attitudes of people for the advancement of their own self-interest.

Finally, the proponents of the method criterion of indoctrination assume that being rational is simply thinking in a certain manner. As we observed earlier, when we talked about the prerequisites, and as we shall see again later, being rational is not just a matter of thinking and acting in a certain manner or form but also a matter of thinking and believing certain things.

THE NATURE OF DOCTRINES

The most common reason given for abandoning doctrinal content as the necessary and sufficient condition of indoctrination is that the term *doctrine* is extremely vague.[15] The problem with that claim, however, is that even if true it would still be a nonsequitur. If the word *doctrine* is vague then that makes *indoctrination* a vague concept but does not constitute a good reason for abandoning doctrine as the criterion of indoctrination.

Very often this claim of vagueness is confused because the real problem is one of ambiguity not vagueness.[16] As I pointed out earlier, words are used ambiguously when it is not clear from the context how they are supposed to be understood. The mere fact that words have variable meanings does not make them ambiguous. We talk, for example, of "sharp criticism," "sharp knives," and "sharp students" without ever getting confused about the meaning of the word *sharp* in these three examples. Let us then adopt a similar approach while we look at the uses of the word doctrine in its various contexts.

The word *doctrine* is sometimes used imprecisely; it is used occasionally to mean *theory* ("Einstein's doctrine of relativity"), *principle* or *policy* ("the Monroe doctrine"), and rarely *rule* ("the doctrine of do unto others...") or *presupposition* ("the doctrine that every event has a cause"). In its plural form the word is used to refer to the teachings of wise persons (e.g., "The Doctrines of Great Educators"). To find out whether the word doctrine is used in any of the above senses we must see if we can substitute these words (*theory*, *policy*, *rule*, or *presupposition*) for the word *doctrine*; if we cannot, then we can be fairly sure that what is being talked about is a real doctrine. The detection of real doctrines does not require special training and skills; only ignorant people would insist that the doctrines of the infallibility of the pope or of the Second Coming are actually theories – such claims might even be considered blasphemous by the faithful because they suggest that the doctrines might be fallible. This rule of thumb will enable us to distinguish doctrines from non-doctrines, but we haven't discussed yet the nature of the doctrines and how they differ from non-doctrines.

The original and proper home of doctrines is religion, and the paradigm cases of indoctrination are to be found in fundamentalist churches and theological seminaries where commitment to doctrines is taken for granted and reinforced. In any other department of human inquiry doctrines are as undesirable as dead rats in the attic. There can be few things as embarrassing to scientists as demonstrating to them that their alleged "theories" are nothing but unfalsifiable doctrines. And there is no canonical repentance available to scientists and others for their mistakes as there might be for religious "heretics." The vague talk about "Marx's doctrines," "Skinner's doctrines," or "Darwin's doctrines" might be intended as criticism of some of the ideas of these men – unless it is simply casual unguarded talk. In such instances the onus is always on the speaker or writer to demonstrate that some ideas of Marx, Skinner, or Darwin are indeed doctrines rather than unclear or unwarranted theories.[17]

THE LITERAL AND THE FIGURATIVE INTERPRETATION OF DOCTRINES

There are two views about the nature of doctrines, which I would like to label the literal or hard view and the figurative or soft view. According to the hard view:

a Doctrines are in principle unverifiable and unfalsifiable beliefs in the literal existence of beings, states of affairs, or relationships. Clear cases of doctrines are the triadic nature of the Christian deity, life after death, and the infallibility of the pope.
b Doctrines are not isolated beliefs but form a system of interrelated beliefs that claims to be the foundation of humankind's "proper" place in the world. This system of doctrines is an all-embracing, totalizing view that encompasses every aspect of human life as subordinate.
c There is a disparity between the linguistic form of a doctrine and its actual function within the system. Although all doctrines are descriptive statements (e.g., "Jesus is the son of God") they have an overriding prescriptive function within their respective contexts. For devout Catholics, for example, the doctrine of the infallibility of the pope is not meant to be an idle belief – they are expected to obey the "infallible" pope. Doctrines, then, are disguised, indirect prescriptions, and their violations are not deemed to be ordinary human errors; within fundamentalist churches or temples they are punishable sins.
d As the last point implies, doctrines presuppose the existence of authorities or institutions that have the power to uphold them when they are challenged by the critics, the heretics, or the faithless and to punish enemies. Without an institution that articulates, orders, and defends them there is nothing that separates them from common superstitions.[18]
e Within all doctrinal institutions and societies the predominant form of communication is monological; inside such groups dialogue and education are severely restricted or distorted by the foundational doctrines.

As will be argued later, doctrines in their literal or their metaphorical sense are outside the rational tradition and, therefore, outside the domain of education. With the exception of some epistemically primordial beliefs (which I have discussed in great detail in the previous two chapters), the only beliefs, outside of religious doctrines, that are unfalsifiable are common superstitions – a reason why many people consider all literal religious beliefs to be nothing more than superstitions. Superstitions, however, are usually isolated beliefs held by individuals and do not have the broad scope and the overriding prescriptive function of religious beliefs. Moreover, the charge of superstition depends on how one interprets doctrines; they can be considered superstitions only if one interprets them to be literal claims, as many people do.

But that is not the only way one can interpret doctrines; there is another soft or metaphorical view of doctrines. According to Wittgenstein, for example, religious beliefs are

> rules of life dressed up in pictures. And these pictures only serve to *describe* what we are to do, not *justify* it. Because they could provide a justification only if they held good in other respects as well. I can say: "Thank these bees for their honey as though they were kind people who prepared it for you"; that is *intelligible* and describes how I should like you to conduct yourself. But I cannot say: "Thank them because, look, how kind they are!" – since the next moment they may sting you. Religion says: *Do this! – Think like that!* – but it cannot justify this and once it even tries to, it becomes repellent; because for every reason it offers there is a valid counter-reason.[19]

Doctrinal beliefs, according to this view, are not ordinary knowledge claims that can be questioned or refuted, nor are they hypotheses, opinions, views, or conjectures that could "possibly," "perhaps," or "probably" be tested, confirmed, or disconfirmed. Anything that we call scientific evidence is, according to Wittgenstein, irrelevant to this interpretation of religious belief. Even the most convincing forecast about the coming of the Day of Judgment would not influence a religious person because "belief in this happening would not be at all a religious belief ... the best scientific evidence is just nothing..."[20]

Although doctrinal beliefs appear to have a referent they are really about something else: "The way you use the word 'God' does not show *whom* you mean – but, rather, what you mean."[21]

"It strikes me," says Wittgenstein, "that a religious belief could only be something like a passionate commitment to a system of reference. Hence, although it's *belief*, it's really a way of living, or a way of assessing life."[22] Confusing religious doctrines with empirical propositions is a blunder that reduces all such beliefs to superstitions. Wittgenstein repeatedly argued that religious belief "not only is...not reasonable, but...doesn't pretend to be" and that it is "ludicrous" to make it "appear to be reasonable."[23] About those who try to make religious belief appear to be reasonable by appealing to facts and evidence, Wittgenstein says that they are unreasonable and that "if this is religious belief, it's all superstition."[24]

The distinction between the literal and the metaphorical views of doctrines sketched above is rarely made by traditional theologians and believers; they usually equivocate by sliding from one into the other, most of the time unwittingly. I think it would be reasonable to claim that, if we accept the above analysis of doctrines, most of what passes as fundamentalist religion today is superstition and should have no place in our educational institutions, unless it is taught as mythology. As literal claims doctrines are common superstitions, and as metaphors they may be important personal perspectives on the world and on human life – and therefore individual subjective preferences and commitments. We do not study Homer in order to find out what the ancient Greek gods were really like just as we do not study Dante's *Inferno* in order to ascertain the veracity of his "map" of hell; these and similar works of literature can find their place in educational curricula not for purposes of religious indoctrination but for their literary value.

DOCTRINES AND THE FOUNDATIONS OF RATIONALITY

It has been argued by several writers that indoctrination is unavoidable in education because it is a prerequisite to the introduction of the young into our rational heritage. Some believe that "the basic assumptions and postulates of an empirical science qualify as doctrines,"[25] whereas others maintain that "indoctrination...has a perfectly good and important role to play in education... Indoctrination may be necessary as a prelude to teaching."[26] Content, according to these writers, cannot be a criterion of indoctrination since the presuppositions of our rational discourse are equally non-rational. But is this all that can be said about the nature of doctrines and the foundations of our rational modes of thinking?

In the remainder of this chapter, I want to show that it is not only what these writers say about doctrines and the epistemic foundations of our thinking but, more importantly, what they overlook that reveals their mistakes and their confused or programmatic intentions; that there is a world of difference between literal doctrines, as I described them earlier, and what Wittgenstein called the riverbed, the axis, the scaffolding, the hinges, and the unmoving foundations of all our thoughts, judgments, language, and actions. In fact, when I have enumerated the important differences it should become obvious that the similarities between them are trivial and inconsequential.

It is never made clear by the above writers what they mean by "assumptions," "presuppositions," "postulates," or "fundamentals" of science. We have identified, however, in chapter 4 and 5 a great number of prerequisite beliefs, virtues, and rules that belong to the bedrock of all our thinking and therefore of science, which are not doctrines. Among these beliefs we can distinguish some that are pseudo-empirical because they are in fact methodological propositions, such as: "Physical objects exist" and "Objects continue in existence when not perceived." There are, next, what I call ordinary certainties such as: "I have two hands," or "I am a human being." These are not propositions that can be doubted, tested, confirmed, and disconfirmed, or about which one can be mistaken. Any attempt to deny such propositions leads to absurdity. As we noted earlier, only insane, mad, demented, or idiotic people, according to Wittgenstein, would express doubt about such propositions, and their doubt would be hollow, senseless, and without consequence. These and similar riverbed beliefs, together with propositions of logic, constitute criteria of rationality about which one cannot be mistaken. A person who insists that his head is stuffed with straw is not making a mistake, he is mentally disturbed. "Being reasonable," says Thomas Morawetz, "is not just a matter of acting and thinking in a certain manner or form but also a matter of thinking certain *things*."[27]

THE DIFFERENCE BETWEEN DOCTRINES AND THE FOUNDATIONS OF OUR THOUGHT

Now that we have sketched the nature of doctrines and the nature of the riverbed propositions that lie at the foundations of all our thinking and acting with reason, we can see more clearly the radical differences between them. First, belief or disbelief in doctrines is not a criterion of rationality, whereas the questioning of riverbed propositions is a sign of organic mental disturbance. A man who doubts that he has two hands while looking at them is not making a mistake, he is mentally sick.

Second, there are countless alternatives to particular doctrines but not to the riverbed certainties. One can doubt, question, accept, modify, or abandon doctrinal beliefs but not riverbed propositions.

Third, riverbed propositions are acquired or inherited without thinking, investigation, or justification; they are not matters of knowledge and must be taught as a foundation, substratum, or background without evidence and without reasons. "Knowing only begins at a later level," says Wittgenstein,[28] when there is "a possibility of demonstrating the truth."[29] Doctrines, on the other hand, are *learned*. There is nothing in human experience that requires us to believe the doctrine of the infallibility of the pope or of the filioque, whereas everything in human experience presupposes the law of induction and the existence of physical objects.

Fourth, whereas all explanations and justifications come to an end, that end is not doctrines that can be doubted and abandoned but the riverbed propositions that cannot. Since riverbed propositions are the foundations of all our thoughts, language, and actions, they must also be the foundations of all our talk about doctrines. It follows, therefore, that doctrines are not at the same epistemic level as riverbed certainties. The onus, then, is on the proponents of indoctrination to show where doctrines belong since they, like all superstitions, are not knowledge claims either.

Finally, a word about the functions of riverbed propositions and of doctrines: while the former enable us to think and act rationally, the latter act as stoppers that control, limit, and channel thought, disallow alternative beliefs, frustrate critical thinking, and distort or corrupt genuine dialogue. That is the reason indoctrination is inherently arbitrary, subjective, and authoritarian: it claims that there are no alternative perspectives on the world and human life whereas, in fact, there are many; it aims at legitimating political authority and power, silencing opponents, and controlling people's lives. The best example of such an institution that I can think of is the Roman Curia of the Catholic Church with its tribunals, congregations, and offices, all of them aiming at preserving and protecting the doctrines of the Church (as they have been formulated throughout its long history) and controlling the behaviour of the clergy and the faithful – all those things that Wittgenstein calls "froth."

THE CONSEQUENCES OF INDOCTRINATION

It must be obvious from the above that indoctrination has profound consequences for the way of thinking and acting of the indoctrinated citizens as well as for the character of their society. At the individual level indoctrination may control and channel people's thinking to such an extent that they come to abhor alternative ways of thinking and behaving. The inculcated doctrines are not isolated beliefs that may be altered by arguments and evidence; they provide a comprehensive view of the world that pervades people's thinking, orders their lives, and renders them incapable or unwilling to entertain the possibility of changing their beliefs and ways of life. In talking about the effects of doctrines on people's lives Wittgenstein makes the following pertinent observations:

> I am not thinking of these dogmas as determining men's opinions but rather as completely controlling the *expression*

> of all opinions. People will live under an absolute, palpable tyranny, though without being able to say they are not free. I think the Catholic Church does something like this. For dogma is expressed in the form of an assertion, and it is unshakeable ... It is not a wall setting limits to what can be believed, but more like a *break* which, however, practically serves the same purpose; it is almost as though someone were to attach a weight to your foot to restrict your freedom of movement. This is how a dogma becomes irrefutable and beyond the reach of attack.[30]

An extraordinary example of this kind of problem is Isaac Newton's unwillingness or inability to change his views about "absolute position, or absolute space, as it was called, because it did not accord with his idea of an absolute God. In fact he refused to accept absolute space, even though it was implied by his laws. He was severely criticized for this irrational belief by many people, most notably by Bishop Berkeley."[31] It must be this foundational position of doctrines that determines a person's way of thinking, that makes them so difficult to dislodge or, as Wittgenstein says, "irrefutable and beyond the reach of attack." This is the reason indoctrinators are interested in inculcating their doctrines in young children as early as possible. They are not necessarily evil; they may be simple-minded, uncritical, and naïve victims of historicized mythologies that aim at "saving the world" from evil – unless, of course, they are motivated by primitive lust for wealth and power and the desire to control people.

Propagandists, however, are always sinister; they know that evidence and rational arguments are powerful in altering people's beliefs and commitments, and so they intentionally pervert them; that is the reason why propaganda has to be fought with sound evidence and cogent arguments. Unlike indoctrinators, propagandists do not abandon evidence; they hide it, misrepresent it, and lie. Indoctrinators, on the other hand, know that if they are successful in inculcating their unfalsifiable doctrines in the minds of the young they will have made them immune to reason, arguments, and alternative beliefs. The political developments in Eastern Europe confirm these points about indoctrination and propaganda. What held the communist regimes in power in these countries was not so much the political quasi-indoctrination but mainly propaganda backed by force; that is why there was the possibility for change in these countries. The Catholic Church, on the other hand, has lasted for centuries and is likely to last for many more because it is founded on doctrines that they inculcate in their subjects.

As I mentioned earlier, one of the reasons we are concerned about indoctrination is that it has serious consequences for the social order. While indoctrinated persons are unable or unwilling to see the subjective and nonrational nature of their doctrines, nonetheless they often want their doctrinal beliefs to function as regulative principles of the way of life of the whole community, if not of the whole world. Their view of the good life and the code of conduct that is embedded in their worldview are predicated on their doctrinal framework that cannot stand public scrutiny on the basis of intersubjective criteria and canons of sound reasoning. By "completely controlling the *expression* of all opinions," as Wittgenstein put it, indoctrination perverts the foundations of our thinking, discourages alternative views, frustrates dialogue and critical thinking, violates our freedoms, impoverishes human life and culture, and divides the world into mindless authoritarian camps; it is indeed the most insidious enemy of genuine dialogue, education, and an open society.

7

The Enemies of Dialogue

There has never been an ideal society of dialogue or education, because there have never existed ideal dialogical citizens and institutions or utopian social conditions anywhere in the world. Genuine dialogue is not fully attainable, and we always fall short of the ideal to some extent. It is obvious, therefore, that we are not after flawless dialogue but only an approximation of it. In every personal relationship and within every institution and society, dialogue is to some extent imperfect, truncated, violated, undermined, corrupted, or deficient; and the causes of these imperfections are within ourselves as well as the nature of the institutions we create and the social conditions under which we live.

OUR PERSONAL CHARACTER

Just as the intellectual and moral virtues are prerequisites of dialogue, the defects in our character and mind are common obstacles to dialogue. Ignorance, thoughtlessness and laziness, lack of discipline and respect for others, the absence of a cooperative spirit, selfishness and greed, racism, dogmatism, lack of clear thinking, and all the other vices undermine dialogue. It may be considered old-fashioned by some people to talk about virtues and vices today, but fashionableness or its opposite cannot be taken seriously in important educational and philosophical discussions. It is encouraging that more philosophers nowadays are recognizing the centrality of virtues in human life and in ethical theory and seeing the limitations of the hierarchical, abstract, and detached theories of deontology and utilitarianism. The correct forms of moral reasoning presuppose as their foundation individual virtues in the same way that rational thinking presupposes all the intellectual virtues, language games, and rules of logic we discussed earlier. General moral principles are inert and lifeless and have no substantial content or motivational force without their particular virtues.

It is our everyday virtues and not our high pronouncements or general moral principles that express our true personal character and our real identity. As I argued earlier, virtues are not like special skills or abilities that we can use if, when, or as we need them. They are unconditional and categorical commitments that constitute our real self, which we cannot neglect, set aside, or abandon at will; to the extent that we do, we fall short of the demands of reason and betray our humanity. It is widely accepted that we call decadent, depraved, inhuman, or even monsters only those who blatantly and repeatedly perform morally appalling, repugnant, and awful acts; not those who don't know their way in the world of mathematics, science, plumbing, hockey, or art. It is because virtues are definitive of personal identity and constitute the foundations of our common form of human life that we choose our friends and partners largely on the basis of their moral character.

THE CHARACTER OF SOCIETY AND OF ITS EDUCATIONAL INSTITUTIONS

There are countless obstacles to dialogue within the political, economic, and social fabric of any society today. The problem is that most of them have become so much a part of our everyday living for so long that we don't see them as problems anymore. Consider, for example, the deceptively innocuous practice of advertising. It is not, of course, as abhorrent and odious as propaganda, but it is usually not a harmless practice either. With regard to its monological character it can compare only to sermons from the pulpit. The purpose of advertising is not to edify, entertain, or comfort us but to sell a product, a policy, an ideology, without any discussion or investigation; any other attributes it may have are only incidental and subsidiary. Most advertising is an aspect of the competitive and exploitative economic and political world that can turn every aspect of human culture into a commodity; it usually appeals to our lowest appetites, which it inflates and reinforces further. It is rarely concerned with our wellbeing, the development of our minds, or the good of society but only with furthering the interests of the persons or corporations it serves. Behind most advertising you will not find necessarily virtuous, caring, and cooperative individuals, companies, or politicians who are concerned about our good, but individuals, political groups, or corporations who want to serve their own interests. If information aims at making us aware of how the world is, advertising aims primarily at misleading us so that with our conditioned and uncritical behaviour we support the interests and appetites of the advertisers. There is very little advertising that aims at merely informing us about our world; most of it serves the interests of the advertisers or their patrons.

Things get worse when we enter the economic and political arenas where insatiable greed and primitive lust for power are the main motivations of individuals, corporations, or political parties. How often do we see politicians inside or outside parliament engaging in genuine dialogue, showing respect for the opinions of others, making honest efforts to understand their opponents, agonizing over whether what they said was true or appropriate, and apologizing for their deceptive statements? The same holds for the competitive world of business, where profit is the ultimate underlying motivation; every other value is secondary. The situation is even worse when we look at international political and economic competition. It appears that the quiet virtues of cooperation, compassion, and understanding, which are at the centre of civilized life, have no place in the aggressive political forum or the competitive marketplace. Here is an example of that deleterious inconsistency. Richard Cooper, an advisor to a former British prime minister said that the challenge for the meta-modern world is to get used to the idea of having two different codes of conduct. While within our society we must obey our laws, when we find ourselves in the jungle we must use the laws of the jungle (*Observer*, 7 April 2002). However realistic this view might seem, it is nonetheless a clear example of a primitive attitude, because it invites us to suspend our moral principles in our international relationships and descend to the level of the primitive – the jungle by definition is lawless. This attitude is a remnant from the old ways of dealing with other people and is part of the problem the modern world must overcome; by renaming this anarchic attitude "meta-modern," Cooper is resorting to mindless and dangerous gibberish. The truth is that the majority of people all over the world believe in the quiet values that are embedded in dialogue and they try within their families and communities to live in accordance with them. Even some of the participants in the relentless rat race get exhausted at the end of the week and go to their temples, churches, or synagogues in order to experience or at least pay lip-service to the quiet values.

The lowest common denominator that is manifested in today's competitive world is not a given in human nature; it is a historical development that can be ameliorated by patient, creative, and inspired multifaceted and comprehensive planning. We must all realize that there are certain political and economic conditions that facilitate dialogue and civilization and others that are inimical to them. In a world of ruthless competition and exploitation, inequality, poverty, fear, violence, uncertainty, and incessant war, it is unrealistic to expect educational institutions alone to bring about a just, cooperative, and open society. The task is enormously complex and difficult and requires long-term planning, patience, and persistence. It requires, among other things, a clear view of what constitutes dialogue (as well as its proper prerequisites and social conditions), which should not be confused with the aggressive and competitive political or economic negotiating, debating, arguing, bargaining, quarrelling, preaching, and haggling that dominate the public world today.

THE INSTITUTIONALIZATION OF THE ENEMIES OF DIALOGUE

Among the innumerable enemies of dialogue have always been institutions and theocratic societies founded on doctrines that systematically violate the prerequisites and principles of dialogue I discussed earlier. The world is divided today, as it has been for centuries, by, among other things, arbitrary doctrines that "legitimize" arbitrary, authoritarian, exploitative, and cruel regimes. There cannot exist genuine dialogue among persons or institutions that are founded on "infallible," absolute, and non-negotiable doctrines; whatever dialogue they may attempt to engage in will be severely limited, circumscribed, or adulterated by their doctrines. As I argued earlier the most pernicious doctrines have their home within monotheistic fundamentalist religions.

The Mystery of Being

Every thinking person recognizes that the world and our life within it are a great mystery. And the mystery is not *how* the world is – science tries to inform us patiently and systematically *how* the word is. The real, inscrutable, impenetrable, and unanswerable mystery is *that* the world and everything in it exist. Why is there anything rather than nothing? To this seemingly genuine question there cannot be any rational answer; and since for all legitimate inquiries there must be, in principle, the possibility of an answer, we may not be dealing with a real question. My view is that this apparently legitimate question is really more like an exclamation, a loud cry or an outburst by which we express our awe or frustration, our disappointment, and our fear: why is there anything rather than nothing! The great mystery begins where our understanding ends.

There is no doubt that, at least at the beginning, the realization that with this exclamation we have reached the boundaries of reason, causes understandable fear and panic in most people. And these emotions that we experience must be among the causes that give rise to mythology and religion; all mythologies and religions attempt to offer "explanations" for our existence and the existence of the world and to give "meaning" to everything, thus putting an end to the mysteriousness of the world and the insecurity and fear that accompany it. That is why at least the three Abrahamic religions represent their god not only as the austere, arbitrary, and almighty creator and overseer of the world who must be feared but also as "our father" or the good shepherd who is looking after our wellbeing.

Cautious, prudent, disciplined, imaginative, educated, modest, and courageous people stop at that great mystery and attempt to find meaning within their present lives, within this common world, and not outside or beyond it; that is, in their everyday interactions with their fellow human beings, in their multiple human relations, activities, and institutions and in scientific, philosophical, historical, or artistic pursuits. These rich cultural activities set the limits of all possible and desirable human engagements and therefore of human reason. Beyond these diverse activities and experiences lies the unknown and for the unknown only the ignorant, the unintelligent, the indoctrinated, the charlatans, and the swindlers speak literally – this is the world of superstition, fantasy, and doctrines. Of course, we can speak metaphorically about anything. Metaphors, however, are neither true nor false, neither correct nor incorrect; we can characterize them only as apt or inapt, appropriate or inappropriate, suggestive or poor, and the like. Later we will talk more extensively about the metaphorical use of language, especially with regard to religion.

Doctrines and the Forms of Knowledge

I made reference to our rational tradition and the demands of reason in previous chapters without identifying explicitly the criteria or standards of rationality. There are two kinds of criteria that underlie our cognitive world: those that govern all our thinking and those that are specific to the various forms of understanding. Among the former we have first the pre-logical ordinary certainties and concepts that lie at the foundation – the riverbed – of all our thought; then there are the rules of logic, the intellectual and moral virtues, and the language games that we have discussed extensively in chapters 4 and 5.

There are, second, the particular criteria of our pluralistic rational tradition that are specific to the various forms of knowledge; our criteria for mathematical understanding, for example, are different from those that are appropriate for our scientific or moral reasoning. In the *Nichomachean Ethics* Aristotle advised us wisely not to demand the same precision in all our inquiries but only the sort that our subject allows or requires. A person who demands from ethics the same certainty and precision that one finds in mathematics is obviously ignorant of the nature of ethical discourse and of the human condition. It is astonishing how often that sensible advice has been overlooked by philosophers; I have in mind particularly the verifiability principle of the logical positivists, which made all non-verifiable statements meaningless, and the claims of the emotivists in ethics that deprived our moral beliefs of any cognitive foundation.

The forms of knowledge we distinguish today did not develop naturally, the way natural objects develop, nor are they gifts from heaven; they are all the human attainments that people have achieved throughout history based on their experience and their interactions among themselves and with their natural surroundings. Although unlikely, nothing precludes the emergence of new forms of knowledge; our cognitive world is open-ended and not predetermined by gods. Those forms we can and should distinguish today are: mathematics and logic, the natural sciences, our moral understanding, knowledge of ourselves and our fellow human beings, philosophical understanding, and aesthetic appreciation. A detailed discussion of the nature of these forms and the complex problems they present is not within the scope of this book; the reason I mention them is that I want to distinguish them from doctrines that do not belong within the rational tradition.

There are two criteria on the basis of which we distinguish between the various forms of knowledge and understanding: a) the peculiar concepts that belong to each form and b) the different methods and principles we use in order to support or evaluate our claims, judgments, and actions. When we talk about the physical world we use concepts such as *object*, *movement*, *weight*, or *velocity*, while when we talk about ourselves or other people, we use words like *person*, *reason*, *decision*, *aim*, and the like. Likewise, when we refer to human actions we characterize them as *just* or *unjust*, *moral* or *immoral*, *courageous* or *cowardly*, and so on. For each form of knowledge we also have appropriate methods and principles by which we establish or evaluate their veracity, reliability, plausibility, worthwhileness, and dependability.[1] In most cases these methods are easily discernible whereas in other cases they are less obvious. Controversies surrounding the logic of particular forms of understanding are not signs of weakness but of vitality and promise, as long as they do not degenerate into arbitrary subjective or idiosyncratic contests. In the natural sciences we have clear criteria for building and evaluating scientific theories; we use observation, experimentation, and induction in order to verify or falsify such claims. In mathematics and logic observation and experimentation are irrelevant; here we use deduction within a system of axioms and examine the logical relationship among various claims. In the world of morals we judge our actions on the basis of fundamental moral principles that, as I argued earlier, are akin to the riverbed of the rest of our thinking.

The enormous problem with all fundamentalist religions is that although their claims have the form of empirical propositions, there are no agreed intersubjective methods for the evaluation of the diverse and very often contradictory claims made by various religions. For that reason their varied beliefs cannot be considered knowledge claims and religion cannot constitute a separate form of knowledge. The fact that in the area of religion we do have specific concepts is not sufficient to classify it as a form of knowledge; that is the reason in religion, when people are careful, they do not speak about knowledge but faith. When scientists disagree about a particular theory they appeal to intersubjective rational standards and methods to support their claims; they don't walk away and establish a "new science" the way religious heretics break away from the old church and establish a new one; science is not a matter of faith, strong convictions, or "infallible" doctrines.

The Political Uses of Doctrines

If we put the numerous religions on a continuum, from the metaphorical left to the literal right, we will see that those that hold a metaphorical view do not talk about god, the hereafter, miracles, and the like literally and do not take seriously the canons of the Church, the hierarchy of the traditional priesthood, and their alleged authority. The metaphorical outlook is a personal, vague, poetic, innocuous, "as if" perspective on life, which is allowed but not required by reason. I can live my life *as if* one day I will have to account for all my thoughts, decisions, actions, and my whole way of life; but I cannot say that sooner or later a god will summon me for questioning – the latter belief is merely superstition. In the same way, when someone says "I thank god for the beautiful flowers in my garden," I understand that they are speaking metaphorically and I conclude that they are grateful. The great advantage of this metaphorical view is that it is both personal and pluralistic and respects other people's ways of living and assessing their lives as long, of course, as they do not violate the demands of reason in any of its forms. The emphasis here is on the gentle virtues of freedom, cooperation, compassion, tolerance, understanding, peace, and justice rather than on rivalry, competition, aggression, violence, and the use of authority. We all seem to need a frame of reference, a vision of how to live our lives, and we ought to be free to choose our own metaphor or symbol, if we need one, and interpret it in our own personal way. There is nothing in this metaphorical view of religious beliefs that violates the demands of reason, the criteria of education, and the principles of dialogue.

On the right side of the continuum are the literalist fundamentalists who believe in an all-powerful personal god, in life after death, severe punishment of sinners, the divine authority of the priesthood, and the other familiar doctrines of monotheistic religions; it is difficult, of course, to imagine how one could hold such beliefs literally just as it is hard to understand people who hold other superstitious beliefs. Unlike scientific beliefs, doctrines are arbitrary subjective inventions that have no relationship to ordinary human experiences; it took the various fundamentalist churches many centuries to develop and order their doctrines out of old myths, to establish their elaborate hierarchies and create their rules, institutional practices, and structures. The cornerstone of all their authority is their doctrines; if you remove those the elaborate institutions and hierarchies collapse. Without doctrines there can be no ordained priesthood, no chains of command, no authoritarian rules, no monologue, no power, and no heretics – all those things that Wittgenstein calls *froth*.[2] In the Middle Ages heretics and "witches" were burned at the stake or excommunicated by the Catholic Church; today there are some Islamic clerics who continue those abhorrent practices of the past. In order for the priesthood to gain power over the people their god must be all-powerful and unforgiving, and we, as inheritors of the "original sin," are condemned sinners who must be saved through the mediation of the Church. The more powerful, unforgiving, ruthless, and vengeful their god is, the more power the priesthood has in controlling the lives of the faithful. And the more sinful we are made to be the more we need their mediation for our salvation. The most widely known and feared slogan of the Catholic Church in the Middle Ages was that outside the Church there is no salvation!

Needless to say, authoritarian institutions such as the fundamentalist churches are among the greatest enemies of dialogue, education, and the open society; they are intolerant of openness, alternative views, doubt, pluralism, and the sense of wonder that are the hallmark of educated persons and of an open and truly democratic society. For as long as I remember there has been talk about dialogue among the churches and even about reunification of Christian churches. But in order to achieve these goals the hierarchies of the churches must be prepared to abandon their "infallible" doctrines and their arbitrary privileges that undermine dialogue; and then they must make serious efforts to engage in a dialogue based on the universal intellectual and moral virtues of humanity that I discussed earlier. So long as they are unwilling to abandon their non-negotiable doctrines and the power these doctrines afford them there is no chance for genuine dialogue, let alone reunion. The fundamentalist doctrines are not just obstacles to dialogue; they are its greatest enemies because they have been fixed and entrenched as the infallible cornerstones of the various religions. In his epistle to the Corinthians, Paul wrote that love is greater than faith or hope[3] – a generous interpretation of that claim would suggest that Paul was trying to emphasize the gentle virtues. The fundamentalists and the televangelists, however, insist in their sermons that without faith we are all doomed; faith gives them authority and control over people, whereas the gentle virtues do away with all that froth.

The preoccupation of fundamentalists with faith and the hereafter alienates believers from real life and the everyday social problems and misdirects them toward the nebulous heavens and the hereafter, as fabricated by the priesthood. It makes people passive and uncritical recipients of meaningless high-sounding slogans and hollow ceremonies that suppress their critical thinking and kill their sense of wonder. The obsession of the fundamentalists with the salvation of their elusive soul leads believers away from the difficult task of nurturing and developing their character, which, if Heraclitus is right, is our powerful "demon"; that "demon" can be nurtured to become our great ally, or can be neglected and turn into our worst enemy. Furthermore, the emphasis on salvation reinforces a form of narcissistic individualism by promoting a personal legalistic relationship with God for the sole purpose of escaping eternal personal damnation and achieving eternal bliss. Compare the prayers of any fundamentalist churches that are preoccupied with faith and subordination to their deity in order to avoid eternal damnation, with the following excerpts from a "prayer" that Johannes Strobaeus[4] attributes to the fourth century AD Neo-Platonist philosopher Eusebius:

> Would that I be nobody's enemy but a friend of the eternal and the permanent ...
> Would that I never quarrel with my beloved ones and if that happens would that I reconcile with them quickly ...
> Would that I never want to harm anyone and if someone wants to harm me would that I escape safely without harming him ...
> Would that I never win a victory that will be harmful to me or to my opponent ...
> Would that I be able to reconcile friends who quarrel and to offer as much help as I can to my friends and all those who need it ...

> Would that I never abandon any friend who is in danger ...
> Would that I respect myself and ... keep under control that which is wild within me ...

How unaffected, natural, compassionate, humane, and thoughtful is this "prayer"; there is no reference to deities, no begging for material or other external goods, no pleading for any kind of nebulous personal salvation – all that the person yearns for is how to protect and improve their moral character and tame the demon within. This anthropocentric view of life acknowledges that we owe our humanity to our society and not to any deities and recognizes that the greatest contribution we can make to society is through the development of our own moral character.

The Undermining of Dialogue and Education

Organized indoctrination by fundamentalist churches aims first at adulterating the prerequisites of dialogue and education by initiating the young as early as possible into arbitrary "infallible" doctrines, as if they were part of the riverbed of our thinking. Their aim at this stage is to inhibit or suppress critical thinking and freedom of thought so that the young embrace the doctrines as if they were genuine prerequisites of thought. It is obvious that there is a fundamental difference between the indoctrinator and the educator: whereas the educator, by trying to secure the genuine prerequisites of our rational tradition, provides the foundations that will enable the development of an autonomous critical thinker, the indoctrinator tries to adulterate the prerequisites with doctrines that usually disable the young forever for rational dialogue and autonomous life; indoctrinators are interested in developing obedient followers for life, not independent critical thinkers.

The war against knowledge that began with the primitive myth of Creation and the Garden of Eden has continued throughout history. According to biblical mythology God expelled Adam and Eve from paradise because of their desire for knowledge. The jealous God of the Bible did not want the man and woman he created to be as knowledgeable as He –

although He created them in His own image. This vengeful, violent, pitiless, fearsome, destructive, racist, and imperialist God (look for these qualities in Deuteronomy, Leviticus, and Zachariah, among other books of the Old Testament) created man so that He would be obeyed, admired, praised, honoured, and worshipped by his subjects. In other words, God planned to create the perfect slave but failed because his creation rebelled against him. Now compare this offensive myth with the myth of Prometheus (discussed in chapter 2); because of "his man-loving disposition," Prometheus tried to empower us with knowledge and understanding and suffered wretchedly for his caring, noble, compassionate, heroic, and benevolent action. How did our world go wrong in accepting the primitive and inhuman myth of the God of the Old Testament and his egotistic behaviour literally, instead of embracing the noble and splendid myth of Prometheus metaphorically?

Of course there is an answer to this question, but an adequate one would require a long treatise; and that is not the purpose of this book. Christianity, which was a Jewish heresy, did not prevail because of its truths or moral superiority; it was imposed by the use of force, systematic fraud, and deception. As Alvin Boyd Kuhn shows, "There is not an iota of history as we know it in the entire Bible,"[5] and as I will try to demonstrate below, even the sound moral rules of the Bible have been corrupted by its theology. The thought that remains after reading the Bible or the Koran is how primitive and uncivilized must have been the societies that created such crude religious codes of conduct and such primitive deities and prophets. It is not surprising therefore that such unsophisticated religions should be so destructive of civilization and so divisive; within Christianity alone there are over one hundred incompatible denominations, each one claiming to have private revelations from God that fit its purposes. The aim of all monotheistic religions is not to create and promote knowledge, understanding, and dialogue but to control people's thinking and behaviour with doctrinaire monologue, threats, and sanctions. They cannot support genuine dialogue and the pursuit of knowledge, because such activities would inevitably undermine the arbitrary authority of the priesthood.

All fundamentalists abandon or betray the demands of reason when it disagrees with their doctrines; and as Plato correctly put it, misologists (haters of reason) inevitably become misanthropists.[6] The number of individuals who have been put to death, jailed, tortured, excommunicated, or anathematized by the organized churches is very long and full of barbarities. Every time scientific inquiry clashed with the prevailing doctrines there was ruthless persecution of free inquiry. Galileo managed to escape with his life, after having been humiliated, but Giordano Bruno and countless others died or suffered at the hands of the clergy. An Iranian professor was sentenced to death recently by the current regime for simply suggesting that every new generation of Iranians should be free to interpret the Koran in its own way rather than rely on old interpretations as definitive and unquestionable. Since 843 CE the Greek Orthodox Church, on "Orthodox Sunday" each year, continues to anathematize (even today) all those who teach Greek philosophy – especially the works of Plato! The current debate in the USA regarding the theory of evolution and homosexuality are examples of the way religious fundamentalism attempts to control freedom of thought, distort our moral code, and corrupt scientific inquiry. Fundamentalist religions do not adulterate only the prerequisites of dialogue and education; they also attempt to undermine the forms of knowledge and understanding that are part of the educational curriculum.

The Distortion of Our Moral Virtues

I do not want to suggest that religions do not make any important contributions to a variety of worthwhile social causes in their respective societies, or that the priesthood consists only of self-aggrandizing, ignorant, or corrupt people. After all, the quiet virtues that I mentioned earlier are part of the code of conduct suggested by all major religions, and many of their faithful, including members of the priesthood, offer invaluable services to their communities and the world. The problem is that their actions are usually conceived and performed under the aegis of their arbitrary, all-embracing, restrictive, and divisive doctrines.

They offer us a code of conduct that is only partly moral; some of it is actually immoral. It is remarkable that all monotheistic religions distort our moral code and adopt the wrong approach to moral education.

Consider first the corruption of the character of our moral virtues. All the character traits that are considered virtues and vices are more or less universal and as old as humanity; it would be very odd to find a society that did not distinguish between the moral and immoral person, the just and unjust, the kind and the unkind, the courageous and the coward, the compassionate and the cruel, the honest and the dishonest, the sincere and the hypocritical, and so on. None of these or other moral virtues owes its existence to religion: human virtues are not foreign to us, do not come from heaven or the minds of prophets or philosophers; they have to do with the human condition and the fact that we are communal animals who are capable of reason. All our virtues and vices have emerged within human communities and are our own collective achievements or failures. It is the social nature of all virtues that is responsible for their measured evolution and subtle variations; it would have been very odd if the diverse social and historical conditions in various cultures had no effect on the character of the virtues present in various societies and historical periods.

Of course our moral virtues have instrumental value, but, as I tried to show earlier, their unique character lies in their intrinsic value: they enable us to be certain kinds of people with certain kinds of character – it is definitional of virtues that they are stable traits of character rather than skills, preferences, or know-hows. Intrinsic value, which is the essence of virtues, is subjugated by all monotheistic religions to the idiosyncratic will of their god and is thus reduced to mere instrumental value. Notice, for example, how, in the Sermon on the Mount, Jesus mentions some virtues (and some morally irrelevant traits of character or conditions such as "the poor in spirit," mourning, and being meek) but then proceeds to assign to them only conditional value by linking them to non-moral ends, thus giving all of them instrumental character. "Blessed are the merciful: for they shall obtain mercy ... the pure in heart: for they shall see

God .... the peacemakers: for they shall be called the children of God," and so on.[7] If all these reward are not sufficient to make you behave prudently, then think of the Day of Judgment, when "the angels shall come forth, and sever the wicked from among the just. And shall cast them into the furnace of fire: there shall be wailing and gnashing of teeth"![8] So if you do not find all the non-moral incentives that Jesus promised sufficient to keep you in line, think of the horrible torture chamber that awaits you! All monotheistic religions use this kind of eschatological terror to make their faithful conform to their code of conduct, thus perverting the nature of virtues. All moral rules of religion are commands from God that must be obeyed; there are no moral problems or dilemmas, no moral doubts, thinking or dialogue; only unthinking obedience to the word of God and his representatives. (In order to see the crudeness of this instrumental view of virtues, imagine yourself lying in a hospital bed when a friend comes to see you with flowers in her hand. You are delighted to see her and thank her for her kindness and friendship but she replies that the real reason for her coming to see you is that she would like to be rewarded in the afterlife and avoid being thrown into everlasting fire!)

As Plato showed us long ago in his dialogue *Euthyphro*, a religious view of moral responsibility in fact destroys the character of morality or renders gods redundant. If the gods command that which is moral then morality is independent and beyond the will of the gods – the gods themselves are obliged to obey the moral principles if they want to be considered moral. There cannot then be any logical relationship between religion and ethics – each person must consider what is the moral thing to do in particular circumstances without appealing to anything outside of ordinary human experience and understanding. If, on the other hand, *moral* simply means what the gods desire and command, then our moral code and reasoning are irrelevant and redundant and the gods become arbitrary and amoral beings: whatever they command becomes moral, and whatever they proscribe becomes immoral! All religions that consider moral rules as commands of their god are at a primitive level appropriate only for perfect slaves. Consider the case of the obedient

Abraham in the Old Testament, who is taking his son Isaac to the mountain in order to sacrifice him to his god because this is what his god has ordered him to do in a dream. How many psychiatrists and lawyers would a modern Abraham need in order to escape from going to jail or be confined to an asylum? Or consider that pitiful pawn Job, who is reduced to a plaything as God and the Devil make a bet, at his expense, whether he will continue to remain a faithful and patient servant to his Master in spite of all the terrible misery and misfortune that the Devil is permitted by God to inflict on him. God wins the bet because Job remains faithful to him, in spite of all his awful sufferings, and is rewarded for being the obedient slave. What this fable teaches is that if people have faith in their god and are patient, without critical thinking, dignity, and self-respect, they will be rewarded simply for being patient and faithful servants; they do not have to possess any other virtues. It tells us also that Job, like Abraham, is a selfish social and political parasite without initiative, pride, freedom, judgment, or self-esteem who does not have to contribute anything to humanity. Once again, it is difficult to imagine how truly primitive must have been the society that produced such dreadful myths for the moral edification of its members. Both Abraham and Job are alien to our sense of what a sensitive, independent thinking and self-respecting person ought to be today. Our hero and ideal example, if we need one, remains the courageous, benevolent and generous Prometheus with his "man-loving disposition."

Any appeal to gods must be considered suspect because it destroys the autonomous character of our moral code; the history of moral virtues is as old as humanity and none of the virtues that humankind recognizes today owes its existence to any religion. It is for this reason that I find it difficult to understand what made Dostoyevsky, over a century ago, warn against the dangers of atheism and saying that without God everything is permitted! Our experience teaches us that the truth is just the opposite: some of the cruellest and most appalling inhuman acts have been and still are sanctioned and performed in the name of God or Allah. As I have tried to show above, all fundamentalist religions pervert or distort our moral code, cultivate intolerance toward other creeds, and divide the world into warring camps.

Is Love a Virtue?

One of the common characteristics of those who have been effectively indoctrinated into fundamentalist faiths is that they usually prefer mental comfort and consolation to clarity and truth. They become indifferent or inimical to rational argument, clear thinking, respect for evidence, open-mindedness, tolerance, and other virtues, when these disagree with their religious beliefs and way of life. Indoctrinated people are unmoved by the demands of reason, are frequently bewitched by vague and high-sounding slogans, and confuse obscurity with profundity. The followers of various religions believe that their faith is superior to that of others; otherwise why should they believe in their doctrines? The truth, of course, is that one rarely chooses one's religion on rational grounds; most believers are born into a community of believers and are initiated into their respective doctrines when they are still very young and incapable of critical thinking and rational choice. As I have argued earlier, the prerequisites of rational thought and judgment are undermined by the inculcation of arbitrary and incomprehensible doctrines.

Among the most common reasons given by Christians for the superiority of their faith is that it is the only religion that preaches love. Every serious student of religion knows that the claim is not true; most religions talk about love and the gentle virtues. The important question, however, is not which religions emphasize love, but whether love is a virtue that can be developed in people; and the obvious and indisputable answer is that love cannot be a virtue for the following reasons:

First, when we look at all the virtues we notice that all of them have their corresponding adjectives; for example: the virtues of kindness and compassion have the adjectives kind and compassionate; justice and benevolence have just and benevolent; philanthropy and generosity have philanthropic and generous. The same is true of the vices. Love, regrettably, does not have a corresponding adjective; and the obvious question is: shouldn't the highest of virtues have its own adjective? Now, it is true that appeal to linguistic phenomena cannot settle philosophical points; it is, however, as Bertrand Russell suggested, an indication of some important truths. Let us see then what the truth is concerning love.

The central point about love is that, like jealousy, hate, pity, and fear, it is not a virtue but an emotion. All emotions are distinguished by their passivity; that is, they are things that happen to us, they are not things that we do. We talk about being possessed by anger, shaken by fear, overwhelmed by grief, or having fallen in love. In all societies people expect their fellow citizens to be truthful, non-malevolent, fair, and cooperative but they can only hope that others will have positive emotions toward them; a husband who demands that his wife love him is both foolish and pitiful. All human actions are accompanied by appropriate emotions, but the emotions have a parasitic character depending on our knowledge, values, expectations, judgments, and the like. Our emotions are immediate and direct evaluations of persons, situations, or objects that do not involve detailed analysis, criticism, and comparison on the basis of explicit criteria and canons of rational thought; they are immediate and spontaneous expressions of our beliefs and character. It is this dependent nature of love that demands that we love only those people we consider fair, sensitive, cooperative, kind, honest, or endearing and not those who are unkind or cruel, hypocritical, or exploitative. It appears then to be insincere, absurd, irrational, and ridiculous to request that we love all people including our enemies, as Jesus is supposed to have said; only rogues, immoral, or demented people can love those who are clearly immoral. It appears then that this call to love everybody is a sentimental smokescreen used by people who are confused or ignorant about the nature, origin, and value of our moral code.

Compare love, which logically cannot be a virtue, with all the gentle virtues of compassion, kindness, generosity, philanthropy, altruism, and mercy; none of them is indiscriminate the way Christian love is – requiring that we love everybody regardless of who they are. Compassionate, benevolent, and generous persons, on the other hand, are always discriminating in the way they practice their virtues: they have a vision of the good life and try to help those individuals who *deserve* to be helped, the institutions and social practices that will likely promote the common good, and so on. Those who love, protect, or abet criminals, villains, or scoundrels are corrupt – these points are matters of clear thinking and common sense. Tolerance, in opposition to love, is a virtue, albeit a provisional one – it depends on whom or what a person tolerates. It is absurd, foolish, and ludicrous to demand love, affection, or even pity from others, but we do have the right to request that others tolerate us so long as our beliefs, values, and way of life do not violate fundamental moral principles; tolerance is one of the virtues that guarantees pluralism, coexistence, and democracy. The doctrinaire fundamentalists, however, while declaring their love even for their enemies, consider tolerance, at best, an inferior virtue; usually they reject it because it opens the way to alternative ways of thinking and living that are inimical to their favourite doctrines.

The Religious Methods of Moral Education

The theory and practice of moral education that emerge from religious mythology have had a long and largely negative effect on our society's understanding of morality and on the way of bringing up children. God, according to the holy books, has given his commands to the prophets, who wrote them down in "holy" books and passed them on to the priesthood; they then pass them on to the parents, who in turn pass them on to their children. The whole process is one of telling, ordering, commanding, and threatening with punishment those who disobey the rigid rules: in other words, the most unimaginative, ineffective, and immoral way of trying to educate the young. As we saw earlier, the most humane and effective way of bringing up children in a civilized society is by example and by dialogical interaction and teaching. And since being an exemplar and having all the virtues and knowledge that moral life and dialogue require is a complex, subtle, and difficult task, people emulate the priesthood and resort to catechism, exhortation, and punishment – that ineffective model is the predominant one in the holy books of all monotheistic religions: tell, threaten, and reward or punish.

Institutions that claim infallibility and use threats and punishments either in their nebulous theologies or in educational practice are not only unsuccessful but also morally wrong. They ignore or corrupt the prerequisites of dialogue and education. They attempt to distort human reason and inquiry in all its forms. They pervert our moral code and create the conditions for closed illiberal societies.

Living with a Sense of Wonder

As I mentioned earlier, it is true that churches, temples, synagogues, and mosques perform many important social functions; I know of no church that does not do some philanthropic work, create a community of believers, provide comfort and assistance to its members, and practice the quiet virtues to some extent. The problem is that most of them put greater emphasis on their doctrines, which sets them up against other equally doctrinaire churches, and, as a result, the gentle virtues are abandoned or take second place; there cannot be genuine dialogue and cooperation among groups each of which is adamant about the infallibility of their respective doctrines from which their code of conduct is derived. The work of the fundamentalist churches is at best contradictory, because it emphasizes these two different and incompatible points of view. Their ceremonies, hymns, and rituals are fossilized, antiquarian, hollow remnants from the past, unrelated and sometimes inimical to the quiet form of life they profess to promote.[9] A clear example of this is the Greek Orthodox Church within which I grew up: its function is primarily ceremonial, ritualistic, hierarchical, and controlling.

In all human activities and institutions there has been considerable development and progress through the centuries, except in the fundamentalist churches where there is no free, creative, and dynamic communal interaction that would result in a continuous improvement of their outlook and an enrichment of their way of life. Those who desire change usually leave the faith or set up their own equally rigid and doctrinaire churches. As long as churches are founded on parochial doctrines they will continue to undermine the development of a rational universal moral code for all humanity; they will continue to pay lip-service to universal moral principles while in their everyday conduct they continue to defend their insular and arbitrary doctrines. Their parochial religious mythologies will continue to divide the world and frustrate meaningful international cooperation and peace. "Infallible" doctrines are the great enemies of humanity not only because they divide the world into unfriendly or warring camps but because they are the most effective stoppers that undermine our capacity to think rationally and to engage in dialogue; they stunt our sense of awe and wonder, diminish our curiosity, and create instead apathetic, inauthentic, submissive, lazy, and bored people. Doctrines predetermine, circumscribe, and limit our thinking and impoverish our lives.

The only promising course of action is to rescue our moral code and our intellectual, aesthetic, and moral sensibilities from the clutches of primitive theocratic institutions; to liberate and repatriate them to our real human communities where we can patiently cultivate the quiet virtues of respect, care, and appreciation for others and their different perspectives and to promote the cooperation and compassionate understanding of our fellow citizens with their particular feelings, ideas, plans, and outlooks. Only in such an environment can we engage in genuine dialogue and in building true human communities, international understanding, and cooperation.

Human activities and perspectives are open-ended: there is no limit to the growth of our intellectual, moral, artistic, political, technological, and practical pursuits – all of human history offers overwhelming evidence of that. The most appropriate attitude toward those human possibilities is one of openness, wonder, awe, astonishment, and curiosity; keeping that sense of wonder unfettered, active, and unconstrained should be one of the central aims of all educational and communal activities, if we want humanity to stay on the path of progress. Unless, of course, contrary to all the evidence and reason, one still believes in the doctrine that the gods have predetermined our nature and our way of life, as all doctrinaire religions preach – in other words, unless one has become what Plato calls a "misologist." "No greater misfortune could happen to anyone than that of developing a dislike for rational argument. Misology and misanthropy arise in just the same way."[10] Since there is not a single valid argument for the existence of a god,[11] all traditional fundamentalist religions are ultimately misologist and misanthropic.

The only hope for existing doctrinaire churches is that they will eventually be transformed and their arbitrary doctrines abandoned or interpreted metaphorically. Instead of worshipping the mythical gods we could celebrate the joy of living and the unity and diversity of humankind; rejoice at the beauty of nature and of our artistic creations and marvel at our scientific achievements and possibilities; delight in our genuine fellowships and friendships and the harmonious human relationships; take pride in our successful social and political institutions and all our communal and individual achievements; offer comfort and support to those who suffer and avoid harming others. Our parochial certitudes and symbols that act as arbitrary stoppers must give place to a universal vision of all humanity in all its diversity and to the maintenance and development of our sense of wonder at our limitless possibilities.

The encouragement of a heightened sense of wonder and the determination not to accept any doctrinal stoppers to our thinking and feeling are probably the most powerful antidotes to all the indoctrination programs worldwide. It would be the best way to transcend our parochial beliefs, nationalities, perspectives, and habits of mind and would enable us to enrich our lives by participating in an open-ended pursuit of human excellences in all their forms and varieties. Instead of confining ourselves within the arbitrary boundaries of our doctrinal beliefs we would be able to experience the unlimited human possibilities that lie between necessity and contingency. It is the most enlightening, motivating, and empowering approach to life; and quite possibly this is what some people mean by *spirituality*. It is not just an intellectual attitude but encompasses our whole being: our thoughts, beliefs, emotions, feelings, values, and judgments – it is a way of being in the world. Far from being an uncertain or threatening adventure, it is the most liberating, joyful, and invigorating way of living one's life.

A strong sense of wonder not only enriches our lives; it protects us from being preoccupied with our private self, which leads to monotony, boredom, dullness, and often hopelessness and despair. It is within the public world of human activities that we find a sense of meaning or fulfillment. A strong sense of wonder must be a powerful motivation to reach excellence not only in intellectual pursuits but also in making us less dogmatic, more conciliatory and understanding, less arrogant and dismissive of sound alternative ideas, more patient and cooperative, more modest and open to dialogue. Embracing the mystery of being and refusing to recommend or accept any non-rational stoppers to our thinking are, in my view, the best guarantees for a free, open, and humane world.

Finally, I suspect that the best teachers are those who have among other traits a strong sense of wonder, which they demonstrate in their everyday interactions with their students. Like other human excellences, demonstrating a sense of wonder would not be a separate subject in the curriculum but an aspect of all excellent teaching and learning.

8

Education, Dialogue, and Human Nature

One could argue that human nature is so complex or unstable or even mysterious that any attempt to reveal its nature and dimensions is doomed; all of philosophy, all the social sciences, and some of the natural sciences are studies of human nature, but they have not been able to offer an adequate and coherent picture. Maybe Heraclitus was right when he opined that "no matter which path you take you will not reach the limits of the human soul because its *logos* is so deep."[1] Perhaps. But we might find that some paths are more appropriate and fruitful than others in shedding some light on our thinking about this important and intractable concept. Maybe we should not follow Heraclitus in the fruitless search for the mysterious depths of the human soul and should try to examine, instead, the various contexts and ways in which we talk about human nature. Our human nature might just lie in plain sight within our ordinary language, beliefs, and actions.

There are important reasons for venturing into such general, "old-fashioned," and obviously ambitious talk about human nature. First, whatever their logical status, appeals to human nature often are among the most persuasive stratagems in educational and other debates. Second, many diverse and even incompatible educational and social policies are defended by appeals to human nature; we must, therefore examine the soundness of such claims. Third, it is often unclear even to those who appeal to human nature what exactly they are committed to and whether their views are tenable. Fourth, some of the most ignominious educational, political, and religious causes have been served by various conceptions of human nature. Finally, appeals to human nature are inescapable; as we shall see later, even those who explicitly claim that there is no such thing, are unsuspectingly committed to some view of human nature.

Appeals to human nature figure as prominently in current educational, political, and religious debates as they have at any other time. In some cases the appeals are explicit, clearly articulated, and defended, while in other cases they are implicit or vague; as we will see later, no educational or political theory can escape from a commitment to some idea of human nature.

When we look at the diverse claims about human nature we see that they are made within different contexts and for different purposes; for example, statements on human nature made in the context of scientific studies of human beings are usually different from those made in political or religious contexts. It would be an impossible and, in any case, pointless task to deal separately with each individual claim. A more prudent and efficient approach would be to attempt to categorize them according to their logical character and then examine the way they might connect up with our thinking about education, dialogue, and human flourishing. The classification that follows does not intend to be either exhaustive or the only possible one; its adequacy should be judged by the extent to which it points out such important connections.

EMPIRICAL STATEMENTS ABOUT HUMAN NATURE

The search for distinct human characteristics is carried on by many disciplines on different levels and for different purposes. Here are two broad classes of empirical claims about human nature.

Human Nature as a Natural "Given"

For a long time psychologists have been looking for the source of all human behaviour in the natural needs or "drives" of the human organism; needless to say, their search has not been a fruitful one. These investigations yielded a very limited number of behaviours (breathing, sleeping, rest, eating, excretion, reproduction), which humans share with all other animals. Although such research is valuable for many purposes, the human sciences would become extremely impoverished were they to limit themselves to the study of such natural givens; the distinction between humans and other animals would disappear as human nature dissolved into animal nature without residue.

Human nature as a natural given is also studied in anatomy, physiology, neurology, etc. These branches of biology examine the structure and functions of the human body often in comparison with a similar study of animals. If by "human nature" we mean those characteristics, attributes, and features by which we ordinarily distinguish between humans and animals, then it is obvious that, whatever hidden biological differences between human beings and other animals are revealed by these disciplines, they cannot constitute the criteria by which we distinguish between human and nonhuman beings in ordinary language; people have been and still are making that distinction without any previous knowledge of such biological differences. For example, whatever the significance of biological findings about the number of chromosomes in humans as opposed to other mammals, the size and complexity of the human brain, the opposable thumb, the complexity of our nervous system, the intricate and decisive role of human genes, and other such differences, they cannot be taken as the only or the most important distinguishing criteria between humans and animals. What these studies establish is that our distinctive biological existence is a necessary condition for being human and that our particular neurophysiological makeup sets certain boundaries to our existence. This way we can distinguish humans from gods, ghosts, phantoms, and other creatures of human fantasy and can check all those who in their ideologies neglect or suppress our necessary biological presence in the world.

The relevance of this aspect of human nature for education is evident. Young people must be protected from those inhuman ideologies and practices that denigrate and smother our legitimate biological needs; not only because the satisfaction of some of these needs constitutes an intrinsic good and a necessary precondition of wellbeing and education but also because their suppression creates all those complex problems that psychoanalysts talk about. On the other hand, the severe limitations of such a concept of human nature for educational theory are also obvious; if educators had to deal with beings that had only a biological presence in the world, the educational task would be impossible. *Ought* still implies *can*, and therefore it would be impossible to set any of our common educational goals for creatures of such limited potentiality. For educational and other purposes, then, the search for human nature could not end with the naturally given.

Human Nature as Culture

The view of human nature shared by social scientists today goes beyond the natural human being. Thus, psychologists do not talk only about "primary drives" but also about "secondary drives" and even about the human mind, cognition, and the emotions; social scientists, on the other hand, talk about culture.

One finds two main streams of thought among many anthropologists and other social scientists, both unsatisfactory. There are those who claim that humans have no nature, they have only history or culture. This group seems to claim that since human nature cannot be identified independent of its cultural expressions, and since there are such obvious differences among cultures, we should dispense with talking about human nature altogether and talk instead about culture or, even better, cultures. These are radical relativists and reductionists who look at humans merely as active, malleable, and adaptive organisms. For these thinkers, human beings alter their own environment through a series of adaptive responses, which in turn shape them. Humans are primarily makers of artefacts seeking to satisfy their biological or socially conditioned needs, desires, and wants – they are not Aristotle's animals who have language and reason or the God-seeking creatures of various religions.

There are others who maintain that if we want to discover what human nature is like we should consider the cultural universals in human history (religion, property, marriage, trade), that is, the various institutionalized ways in which human beings organize their lives and come to terms with the world. The task, then, is to identify these assumed cultural universals. It is not very clear, however, what this kind of study will yield and why we should label its findings "human nature." The first problem is that these "fake universals,"[2] as A.L. Kroeber called them, are vague categories; how do we determine what is religion, property, trade, and the like? All one has to do is to compare the institutions, values, and customs of any Western nation with those of Stone Age humans. The second problem is that, although the comparative study of human institutions, values, etc., does shed light on the human condition, there is no compelling reason to assume that what is distinctly human will inevitably manifest itself evenly in every culture, regardless of the conditions that influence the institutions, practices, beliefs, customs, and values of a society. What these cultural regularities tell us is how human needs, desires, and values come together to form the specific communal institutions and practices in order for humans to cope with the complex configurations of diverse conditions in particular times and places. Finally, it is quite likely that those who attempt to define human nature in terms of some common empirical regularity may be appealing to the lowest common denominator of the human condition. Since all conceptions of human nature may function sometimes as self-fulfilling prophecies, the proponents of this approach may be promoting mediocrity. There is always the danger of mistaking human nature as a rigid and fixed natural given rather than as an emerging and evolving human achievement.

The empirical study of the particular character of a culture is fundamental to educational planning. It establishes, among other things, the contingent parameters within which one can set suitable objectives, organize the appropriate content, and select suitable methods and institutional arrangements to educate the citizens. In spite of all this, however, such empirical studies by themselves cannot provide the educational criteria and principles that are needed for determining the character, content, and values of educational policy and practice.

To what extent there are alternative cultural institutions for civilized forms of human life is an important empirical question that cannot be ignored. The real danger that we have to guard against is when certain obvious false universals, such as religion, are presented as constitutive of human nature in order to serve dubious ideologies. We have, in such cases, the most common programmatic and, as we will see below, pernicious definitions of human nature.

PROGRAMMATIC STATEMENTS ABOUT HUMAN NATURE

Some of the statements about human nature that have been most influential in educational and political theories are not empirical claims. They are programmatic statements that are at the foundations of political or religious ideologies and have a powerful prescriptive function within them; their nature depends on the ideology they are designed to serve. Although political and religious programmatic definitions of human nature have many similarities, I would like to discuss them separately because the first pretend to be theoretical claims that can be refuted, whereas the second are clearly irrefutable religious doctrines that are considered infallible. Recognizing a particular claim in political theory as a doctrine is an embarrassment that leads to its abandonment, whereas the foundations of all fundamentalist religions are constituted of doctrines.

Political Statements on Human Nature

In my opinion the most articulate, powerful, and influential political programmatic statement of human nature is to be found in Plato's *Republic*. His view of human nature is clearly and brilliantly modelled on his rigidly stratified political community. The tripartite division of the human psyche (the rational or reflective, the spirited, and the appetitive elements) mirrors a parallel stratification in the state: the rulers who will govern the state, the auxiliaries who will defend it, and the producers who will provide the material goods. The excellences that should characterize each one of the three classes of citizens are the same ones that should be found in the harmonious psyche of each citizen, that is, wisdom, courage, and temperance. Justice, the fourth excellence, is present in the community when each class performs its appointed function well and does not interfere in the work of the other classes. The same excellence is present in the individual psyche when its three parts perform their own functions properly and harmoniously. In other words, the public politics of the community is the model for the inner politics of the psyche.

One cannot help but admire Plato's ingenious political theory and his symmetrical stratification of the state and the human psyche, which is, however, based on "one noble lie" or a myth, as he himself states in the *Republic*.[3] Here is Plato's tale that he plans to tell all the citizens of the Republic:

> While all of you in the city are brothers .... yet god in fashioning those of you who are fitted to hold rule mingled gold in their generation, for which reason they are the most precious – but in the helpers silver, and iron and brass in the farmers and other craftsmen.[4]

It is not my aim here to inquire into the reasons for Plato's low view of human nature, which leads him to the limited and inflexible stratification of the members of the Republic. Neither is there any intention to reconstruct and evaluate his political or educational theory. What I want to point out here is that his view of human nature was politically motivated and that not all its implications for education, as Plato "derived" them, are educationally desirable.

Plato's overriding concern for permanent order and stability in the state forced him to cast individual citizens into rigid social classes with very little mobility or even possibility for dialogue and growth. His preoccupation with political stability in the *Republic* leads him to elevate the principle of specialization and make it central to morality. Individual freedom, choice, and self-expression are ignored or discouraged. The inflexible hierarchical structure of the state does not allow the citizens to see themselves from varied social perspectives and to interact with others freely. Most of the citizens are to be indoctrinated and trained in order to perform their limited roles and be content with them. Education and rational dialogue seem to be reserved for those select few in whose nature god "mingled gold"; Plato's political and practical educational policy trumps his epistemology, which we find in his brilliant allegory of the cave in the *Republic* – true education is reserved for only some citizens who, as he says, are "most precious." It is ironic that the philosopher who wrote his philosophical works in dialogical form discourages genuine dialogue in the Republic because of his preoccupation with the stability of the social order.

All this does not mean that Plato was not one of the keenest educational and social theorists and planners of all ages – there is no important aspect of education that escaped his attention. The problem is that, by making education totally subservient to the political goals of the state, Plato ignored the important distinctions between education, training, socialization, and indoctrination, and he limited education for very few citizens. The "noble lie" mentioned above is only one instance of that attitude in Plato. Even his remarkable new idea about individual differences among people suffers from his overriding political commitments; the categories are very limited, rigid, and purely prescriptive. His tripartite categorization of citizens precludes or at least restricts dialogue among them and lays down the grounds for a possible closed society.

Religious Statements on Human Nature

Religious statements on human nature are not unlike other demeaning views of human nature that seek to control human beings. But they should be treated separately because of their explicit connection with religious mythologies and their arbitrary, absolute, and authoritarian character; they are not matters of imperfect theory but of doctrine. Perhaps the most arbitrary and pernicious programmatic view of human nature is to be found in the Old Testament and in Judeo-Christian theology. According to Genesis, although man was created in the image and likeness of God, he sinned by disobeying the Almighty and as a result was cursed by God and thrown out of Paradise. That was Adam's original sin; it seems that Adam is here portrayed as a kind of corporate man representing all future human beings, since, according to traditional Christian theology, all of us share in Adam's sin. Baptism is intended to free us from this primordial sin and restore our lost innocent condition, but not all the fathers of the Christian churches agree on its effectiveness. Humanity has been vacillating between good and evil since Adam and Eve declared their freedom and personal choice by eating of the forbidden fruit. The relative strength of these two aspects of human nature varies according to the doctrinal dictates of the various Christian sects or heresies. We find one of its first formulations in St Paul. The Aristotelian concept of *akrasia* (weakness of the will), which is part of the human predicament, is cast by Paul in dramatic theological terms; he describes the unremitting conflict in the following way:

> In my inmost self I delight in the law of God, but I perceive that there is in my bodily members a different law, fighting against the law that my reason approves and making me a prisoner under the law that is in my members, the law of sin. Miserable creature that I am, who is there to rescue me out of this body doomed to death?[5]

A generous critic might say that Paul is merely putting an innocuous religious garment on a universal human predicament (akrasia) without altering its nature or the ways we ought to cope with it; it is just a personal metaphorical way one might talk about an indisputable human problem – Paul's argument does not gain any rational strength by identifying human reason with the law of God. In addition to divine assistance, according to Paul, education is supposed to facilitate the work of the law of God in its struggle against the law of sin. The character and function of education depends on the relative strength of these two components of human nature. It should be noted, however, that Paul narrows the problems of choice to that between the demands of reason and those of the body, as if all the morally wrong temptations are those of the body. The additional problem is Paul's identification of the demands of reason with those of his God, that is, with the arbitrary and conflicting views of the prophets and the Church fathers through whom their God always speaks.

Perhaps the most irrational and politically insidious version of the doctrine of the original sin is to be found in another "Saint" of the Christian church, Augustine. According to Augustine, Adam's original sin corrupted and transformed not only human nature but the whole of nature; not only did it make us mortal, subject to all sorts of miseries, but it also changed the structure of the universe and made the world an unfriendly, dangerous, and difficult place to live. The forbidden fruit, according to Augustine, is a symbol of personal freedom, autonomy, and independence, which are vices, whereas the ultimate virtue is absolute obedience to God. Adam's sin made the human condition a kind of disease and "validated" the Christian Church's absolute authority to treat us as its sick patients; with the help of Augustine and other Church fathers it also became eventually an imperial religion. The autocratic, jealous, and amoral God of Augustine allowed us to sin in order to show us that our "true good is free slavery" to Him and to his agents, the hierarchy of the Church, and ultimately to the emperors and kings that the Church supported.[6] "Human beings cannot be trusted to govern themselves, because our very nature – indeed all nature – has become corrupt as a result of Adam's sin."[7] Augustine's God is to be obeyed, worshipped, and feared by His subjects; disobedience means eternal damnation and punishment. The horrific eschatological terror of Augustine's arbitrary and inhuman theology translates into a justification of the absolute political power of the representatives of the Almighty, who are the Church fathers and ultimately their favourite political leaders. The more pervasive and devastating the nature of our sin, the more terrifying is the power of God and, therefore, of the Church hierarchy.

Belief in the myth of the "original sin" is like an untreatable virus that distorts and corrupts all human thinking and makes human reasoning, education, and dialogue undesirable. All our attention must be directed to finding the will of the whimsical God and obeying Him; human freedom, autonomy, self-esteem, personal judgment, and choice are to be abandoned as vices. Augustine laid the foundations of a totalitarian ideology that oversees and controls not only the code of conduct of its followers but also all their thoughts, beliefs, outlooks, and emotions. Our material existence was denigrated and disparaged and became only a source of guilt and suffering in the only life available to us. I cannot imagine a more arbitrary, outrageous, evil, destructive, deceitful, and cynical view of human nature.

Similar negative and depressing views of human nature are at the foundations of all closed illiberal and impoverished societies that are opposed to freedom of thought and choice, mistrustful of human reason, critical thinking, and autonomy, inimical to openness, pluralism, and genuine dialogue, and supportive of authoritarian regimes. All such negative or pessimistic views of human nature demean human dignity, pervert every attempt at genuine dialogue, undermine education, and put sinister constraints on human civilization.

Progressive Views of Human Nature

These pessimistic views of human nature have had numerous adherents among social and educational theorists and have influenced many important institutions in our society. Effective reaction against such views came rather late. Perhaps the strongest early critic of such views was Jean Jacques Rousseau, who in his *Emile* declared:

> Let us lay down as an incontrovertible rule that the first impulses of nature are always right; there is no original sin in the human heart, the how and why of the entrance of every vice can be traced.[8]

According to Rousseau human nature is good, it never deceives us; it is society's evils that alienate us from our good natural selves. It was this romantic programmatic character of Rousseau's claim, in the context of the inhuman formalism and rigidity of his times, that made it such a timely, powerful, and liberating slogan. There has been hardly any educational reformer who has not been influenced by the positive and optimistic views of Rousseau; Pestalozzi, Froebel, and Montessori, the child-centred educational theorists, the humanistic psychologists and educators have all been affected by this refreshing new idea of human nature and the nature of childhood.

The influence of this affirmative view of human nature on educational thought is obvious in the following statement by Abraham H. Maslow:

> Since this inner (human) nature is good or neutral rather than bad, it is best to bring it out and to encourage it rather than to suppress it. If it is permitted to guide our life, we grow healthy, fruitful, and happy. If this essential core of the person is denied or suppressed, he gets sick sometimes in obvious ways, sometimes in subtle ways, sometimes immediately, sometimes later.[9]

It must be obvious that, although this optimistic and beneficial reaction against the traditional pessimistic view of human nature and the misconceptions about the nature of childhood was greatly needed, the claim that human nature is good is also a vague programmatic slogan. How else is one to interpret Maslow's claim that "this inner nature is good or neutral," or Rousseau's declaration that "the first impulses of nature are always right"? Nothing in nature can be said to be good or right in itself outside human interests, needs, and norms. Even Rousseau recognizes this point when he talks about the child's selfishness. The child's "self-love," he says, "only becomes good or bad by the use made of it and the relations established by its means."[10] A more serious problem with Rousseau's initial view is that it fails to recognize the complex social dimensions of the self and its multiple interactions within each human community; it is only within such communities that human nature emerges and develops. Its proponents seem to overemphasize the individual aspect of human thought and action and ignore the social, intellectual, and cultural achievements of humanity and all the norms, virtues, perspectives, standards, and tastes embedded within them.

The purpose of this section is not to offer a detailed evaluation of these broad political, religious, or educational views of human nature but simply to point to their programmatic intentions; they involve serious political choices, masquerading as empirical claims. To put it differently, they are decision statements that act as stoppers in the search for justification and explanation of human actions, choices, beliefs, policies, and institutions. While they may perform a very useful function, as Rousseau's views did, they must be understood for what they really are, i.e., programmatic or persuasive reactions against policies and practices deemed undesirable; attempts to remedy social or educational evils or calls for changing our views, practices, and beliefs.

IS THERE HUMAN NATURE?

There are many people today who believe that there is no such thing as human nature, that all such claims have programmatic intentions. I have chosen to discuss two such typical views that represent those that are fashionable today. In my opinion, the view that there is no human nature makes sense only as an awkward reaction against particular religious or political views of human beings such as those I discussed above.

The first example of the deniers of human nature is Jean-Paul Sartre, who argues:

> there is no human nature, since there is no God to conceive it. Not only is man what he conceives himself to be, but he is also only what he wills himself to be after this thrust toward existence. Man is nothing else but what he makes of himself.[11]

The assumption that seems to be hidden behind this claim is that we can talk about human nature only if it is some kind of a "given" – either a gift of God or of nature. But what Sartre is actually doing (we can ignore his non sequitur in the first sentence) is rejecting one view of human nature and replacing it with another. Humans, according to Sartre, are the only beings aware of themselves, unlike "a patch of moss, a piece of garbage, or a cauliflower." A human being is capable of perceiving alternatives and choosing freely and, therefore, "is responsible for what he is."[12] But in that case, not only do humans have a distinct nature, it appears that this nature is a noble and demanding one; humans are free to define themselves and thus they are responsible for their choices and actions. Human nature is not a natural given or a gift of the gods, it is a human achievement, and we, therefore, are responsible for what we become. But if our nature depends on our conception of ourselves and our own choices, then we must take into consideration not only our own genetic endowment but, above all, the nature of the culture into which we are born; there are limits to what we can "will" and how we can "conceive" ourselves and, therefore, what we can "make" of ourselves.

Any talk about human nature requires us to describe the nature of the world we inhabit, about which Sartre does not say much. Michael Oakeshott provides us with that necessary element, missing from Sartre's view. Unlike other animals, Oakeshott says, we are born into a world of beliefs, values, norms, expectations, visions of the good, etc; it is only within such a world that we can be the choosers that Sartre claims we are or ought to be.

Sartre's claims about human nature without Oakshott's are seriously lacking. Oakeshott's strategy, initially, is not unlike that of Sartre; he also denies categorically that we have a nature, but this only in order to present us with a view of human nature that is as rich and complex as human history and culture. Oakeshott argues:

> Man is what he becomes; he has a history but no "nature." This history is not an evolutionary process or a teleological engagement; there is no "ultimate man" hidden in the womb of time or prefigured in the characters who now walk the world. Human beings pursue satisfactions which they believe to be desirable, but human conduct is not the flowering of a settled potentiality.[13]

What Oakeshott is correctly rejecting in this paragraph is the romantic view of naturally unfolding human tendencies and flowering potentialities – a view that is still fashionable today. He then proceeds to offer numerous characterizations of human experience that are necessary for any serious account of human nature. Although Oakeshott's initial point is not unlike Sartre's, he proceeds to tell us a great deal more about the character of the world that we humans inhabit, which is also the locus of human nature:

> Human beings are what they understand themselves to be; they are composed entirely of beliefs about themselves and about the world they inhabit. They inhabit a world of intelligibles ... Being human is recognizing oneself to be related to others, not as the parts of an organism are related, nor as members of a single, all-inclusive "society," but in virtue of participation in multiple understood relationships and in the enjoyment of understood, historic languages of feelings, sentiments, imaginings, fancies, desires, recognitions, moral and religious beliefs, intellectual and practical enterprises, customs, conventions, procedures and practices; canons, maxims and principles of conduct, rules which denote obligations and offices which specify rules ... To be without this understanding is to be, not a human being, but a stranger to the human condition.[14]

Oakeshott not only has given us what are the essential characteristics of being human but also the important conditions that make education possible. Human beings are born into a world of beliefs and meaningful, understood relationships, languages of feelings, and imaginings. Without a regular interaction with their culture, humans could not develop their human characteristics. It is this fact that gives our experience a distinctive human quality, enables us to live in communities, and facilitates the development of our mind and character. To say that humans are rational and dialogical social animals comes to the same thing.

UNIVERSAL BELIEFS ABOUT HUMAN NATURE

Given the richness of human nature, as described by both Sartre and Oakeshott, one wonders what was it that they meant by "human nature," which they both went on to deny? Did they merely want to suggest the obvious, namely, that human nature is not a preprogrammed natural given that is present in the newborn and unfolds according to natural or teleological laws? Were they reacting against the claims of some psychologists who during that period used to talk about basic needs or drives as definitive of human nature? Or did they mean that one can talk about the universal features that determine the character of human experience but deny that there is a common content in the beliefs, and practices held by different people or different societies? It is obvious that many of the particular beliefs and practices of all societies are contingent on particular historical, geographical, economic, and political conditions. In that case the content of a particular society's beliefs could be significantly different from that of other societies, but not its general characteristics as described by Sartre and Oakeshott.

As we saw earlier, the view that different cultures may have different beliefs and practices and therefore different human natures is the most common but superficial claim of cultural relativists, who confuse descriptive relativism with normative relativism. Appeals to relativism in such cases function as stoppers in the search for explanation and understanding of significant differences among societies. The appropriate question for the open-minded researcher is: which conditions might be responsible for the different beliefs and practices in different societies? Human beings are not born nor do they operate in a social vacuum but are influenced by an enormously complex set of circumstances in every society and period of history. Our human mind and our personality and character are not determined exclusively by the properties of the individual genes in our body; just as one cannot explain human dancing in terms of our muscles, one cannot explain mind in terms of our genes. It would be surprising if all human beings spoke the same language and held identical beliefs about the world and themselves in spite of the different conditions surrounding them or the different time periods they lived in. Yet, what is clear and astonishing is that all human beings, in spite of their varied circumstances, do share an enormous number of universal beliefs. It is in large part because of these universal beliefs and practices that Western anthropologists can live in and study the most diverse and exotic cultures without going mad.

Here are some of these beliefs that all humans share. All human beings believe that they exist, have a body with limbs, a head and sense organs that enable them to perceive the world and the numerous causal relationships within it; that they have needs, desires, appetites, tastes, likes and dislikes, thoughts, intentions, ambitions, joys, and sorrows; that other people exist, similarly equipped; that there is a world of objects, plants, minerals, and animals, some of which they and other humans use for their needs; that all human beings are vulnerable (may be injured, constrained, betrayed, insulted, ridiculed, or killed), fallible (make mistakes in perception, judgment, choices, planning, acting, and the like), and have limited knowledge, skills, aptitudes, talents, capacities, and virtues; that all humans are born in need of care due to their physical, social, and intellectual immaturity; that all humans, as members of society, may have conflicting desires, wants, interests, needs, obligations, and aspirations; that all humans communicate through language and can be informed, guided, corrected, and admonished or misinformed, misguided, deceived, and misled; that all humans experience passions, feelings, and emotions such as fear, shame, pride, envy, pity, anger, love, hate, or jealousy; that no humans can avoid situations where they have to choose between alternative beliefs, suggestions, rules, plans, courses of action, and the like; that newborn children cannot have any of these beliefs, which they acquire or learn as they grow up within human communities. Most of these are prerequisites that we acquire, but some are matters of knowledge that we learn.

These and countless other beliefs hold universally with regard to human beings: they are not about particular roles, tasks, rules, laws, conventions, preferences, agreements, or contracts that can be changed at will, or about beliefs or ways of life that can be abandoned. Whatever their epistemological status, the important point about these claims is that nobody can be exempted from them without, at the same time, seriously risking their status as human beings. On the other hand, there are other universal characteristics that are not essential to being a human being.

The importance of recognizing these universal truths about human beings lies in the fact that they set the boundaries of human possibilities and, consequently, the boundaries of our moral code and our social and educational policies. Given the way we and the world are, there are limits as to what we can say about ourselves and the world. We cannot say, for example, that we plan to abandon or eliminate universal gravity, have a serious dialogue with our favourite houseplants, or invite Socrates to dinner. *Ceteris paribus*, human beings cannot be said to want to be enslaved, confined, tormented, starved, distressed, injured, offended, or deprived of their health. Finally, newborn children cannot perform any of the countless language games that adults perform, such as describing, agreeing, promising, or explaining.

These examples suggest that being human is neither the result of natural development nor is it a divine gift; we become humans through early initiation into the prerequisites of human development, while with education we further develop our mind and character. We are born with the potentiality to become humans; we are, as it were, born at the threshold of humanity, but not at our destination – and it is the business of early childcare and education to help us achieve our full humanity. As Oakeshott put it:

> If a human life were a process of growth in which a potential became an actual, or if it were a process in which an organism reacted to its circumstances in terms of a genetic equipment, there would be no room for a transaction between the generations designed expressly to initiate a newcomer into what was going on and thus enable him to participate in it. But such is not the case ... In short, the educational engagement is necessary because nobody is born a human being,

> and because the quality of being human is not a latency which becomes an actuality in a process of "growth." The human newcomer is not an organism in search of an accommodation to circumstances favorable to its continued existence; he is ... a creature capable of learning to think, to understand and to enact himself in a world of human enactments and thus to acquire a human character.[15]

THE PRINCIPLES OF RATIONALITY AND HUMAN FLOURISHING

For the above universal claims to be true, then, human beings must have the capacity to perceive the world according to some categories, remember their various impressions, and appraise and judge them according to relevant criteria. The performance of any of these intellectual acts presupposes certain principles of rationality such as truth-telling, respect for evidence, coherence, consistency, and non-contradiction. As we saw earlier, there is no question of choosing, preferring, or selecting these principles, because they are presupposed by any cognitive claim we make; they are at the foundations of all our thoughts and actions and permeate all the forms of human experience: perceptions, judgments, choices, even feelings and emotions. As R.S. Peters aptly put it, "human life is a context in which the demands of reason are inescapable."[16] The principles of rationality are relevant whenever we report an occurrence, describe our emotions, justify our suggestions, classify information, evaluate an argument, explain a theory, or choose a course of action. As Peters states again:

> Man is thus a creature who lives under the demands of reason. He can, of course, be unreasonable or irrational; but these terms are only intelligible as failings short in respect of reason ... the demands of reason are not just an option available to the reflective. Any man who emerges from infancy tries to perceive, to remember, to infer, to learn, and to regulate his wants. If he is to do this he must have recourse to some procedure of assessment ... To say, therefore, that

> men ought to rely more on their reason ... is to claim that they are systematically falling down on a job on which they are already engaged. It is not to commit some version of the naturalistic fallacy by basing a demand for a type of life on features of human life which make it distinctively human.[17]

In order to avoid this systematic "falling down" in their essential human character the young must be guided from the beginning to see clearly the various demands of reason that are embedded in all intellectual and moral virtues and all language games and abhor any practices that violate them. And they must also learn all those things that are allowed by reason, such as hobbies, tastes, preferences, and all the metaphorical ways of talking about our lives that I mentioned earlier. It is not a question of turning inward to their unformed and chaotic consciousness, or turning outward to the world of nature – as some educational slogans suggest. The young must form first the prerequisites for such explorations. These prerequisites are formed as the young participate in genuine human relationships and learn to take things as we do. As children come to learn language and sort out their first broad categories and distinctions, they also learn the principles of rationality that are presupposed by such human activities as well as the intellectual and moral virtues that are embedded in each language game. They learn to distinguish between reality and fantasy, true and false beliefs, relevant and irrelevant evidence; they also learn the value of consistency, clarity, and objectivity. Equally important for their development is the cultivation of those dispositions, habits, skills, attitudes, character traits, and virtues that are required for the implementation of the principles of rationality within the various forms of human experience. It is only under such conditions that we can expect human nature to flourish in all its important educational dimensions.

I have argued throughout this book that we must view education as dialogue. Understanding education as dialogue enables us to see, first, the fundamental importance of the prerequisites of educational development (ordinary certainties, rules of logic, intellectual and moral virtues, and language games), which constitute the foundations of all worthwhile human development. Second, it emphasizes clearly and convincingly the non-instrumental value of education by pointing out the central place of its intellectual and moral prerequisites. Third, it places education in the public world of the intellectual, moral, aesthetic, and social achievements of humanity. Fourth, by demarcating the prerequisites that constitute the foundations of all our thinking and acting with reason, it enables us to distinguish justified true beliefs from doctrines, superstitions, and other forms of human failures and to detect the various ways in which education and civilization can be undermined.

We now have the reasons on the basis of which we can reject as misleading all programmatic views of human nature and education. The aim in education is not to prepare workers to keep the wheels of industry turning, or citizens who will surf the internet and defend their country, or the religious devotees who will dedicate themselves to their faith. Although educated persons may choose any of these roles, they do not have to if such roles threaten the foundation of civilized life. The aims in education cannot be defined in terms of roles, functions, conventions, or institutions, just as human nature cannot be defined in terms of the bogus universals of cultural anthropology. It should not be surprising that the conditions for the proper flourishing of human nature are also the conditions for genuine dialogue and education. As Democritus observed long ago, "Nature and teaching are similar, for teaching transforms men, and as it transforms them, it creates nature"[18] – if of course it is guided by the criteria of education discussed earlier. Education can best be seen as an engagement in a civilized dialogue among the generations designed to initiate all newcomers into a worthwhile form of life and thus enable them to participate in it and realize their desirable human potential. Like the concept of education, the concept of human nature is vague and open-ended; neither of them can be a specific objective that can be reached but an ideal that can be only approximated.

Notes

CHAPTER ONE

1 Plato, *Theaetetus*, 155 d.
2 Aristotle, *Metaphysics*, I, ii. G.
3 Wittgenstein, *Philosophical Investigations*, #329 (Hereafter *P.I.*).
4 Wittgenstein, *Lectures and Conversations*, 2 (italics added).
5 Wittgenstein, *P.I.*, #432.
6 Wittgenstein, *Zettel*, #173.
7 Cavell, *Must We Mean What We Say?*, l19.
8 Wittgenstein, *P.I.*, #384.
9 Ibid. #111.
10 Ibid. #122.
11 Ryle, "Philosophical Arguments" in *Logical Positivism*, A.J. Ayer (ed.), 336.
11 Wittgenstein, *P.I.*, #119.
12 Ibid.
13 Waismann, *The Principles of Linguistic Philosophy*, 3-4.
14 Ryle, "The Theory of Meaning" in *Philosophy and Ordinary Language*, Charles E. Caton (ed.), 153.
15 Austin, "Other Minds" in *Philosophical Papers*, 44-84.
16 Strwason, "Construction and Analysis" in *The Revolution in Philosophy*, Ayer et al., 107.
17 Wittgenstein, *P.I.*, #116.
18 Ibid., #18

19 Ryle, "Ordinary Language" in *Ordinary Language* in V.C. Chappell (ed.), 38.
20 Wittgenstein, *P.I.*, #120.
21 Austin, "A Plea for Excuses" in *Philosophical Papers*, 132-3.
22 Ibid., 130.

CHAPTER TWO

1 Peters, "What Is an Educational Process?" in *The Concept of Education.*
2 McClellan, *Philosophy of Education.*
3 Wittgenstein, *P.I.*, 1953, #571
4 Ibid., #150.
5 Ibid., 59 (a) and (b).
6 Wittgenstein, *Lectures and Conversations*, 8.
7 Heraclitus, *Fragment* 50.
8 Ibid., *Fragment* 119.
9 Plato, *Apology,* 38a.
10 Plato, *Theaetetus*, 152a.
11 Sophocles, *Antigone*, 330
12 Aeschylus, *Prometheus Bound*
13 Heraclitus, *Fragment*, 40
14 See *Paideia: The Ideals of Greek Culture*, vol. 1.
15 Quoted by Haack, *Manifesto of a Passionate Moderate*, 32.
16 Whitehead, *The Aims of Education*, 19.
17 Peters, "Aims of Education – a Conceptual Inquiry" in *The Philosophy of Education*, 20. See also his *Ethics and Education.*
18 Dewey, *Democracy and Education*, 76.
19 Whitehead, op. cit., 13.
20 Aristotle, *Metaphysics*, 9.

CHAPTER THREE

1 In my discussion of *education* and *aims* I am indebted to the pioneering work of R.S. Peters. In addition to the works referred to below I would like to mention *Ethics and Education* and "The Justification of Education," in *The Philosophy of Education.*

2 Unlike descriptive definitions, which are explanatory, programmatic definitions are recommendations that aim at influencing social practice. As Israel Scheffler says: "Programmatic definitions ... may be used to express serious moral choices" *(The Language of Education*, 21). For examples of serious programmatic definitions, see Scheffler's discussion of *teaching* in above and Komisar, "Teaching: Act and Enterprise," in *Concepts of Teaching: Philosophical Essays*, Macmillan and Nelson (eds). For an examination and criticism of such approaches to the analysis of *teaching*, see Kazepides, "Wittgenstein and the Rationalists on Learning and Teaching."

3 Compare this statement with Hugh Socket's claim that aims statements "are to be regarded as *definitional* of an institution in that they *describe* what the institution *is for* and thus what it *is*" ("Curriculum Aims and Objectives: Taking a Means to an End," *Proceedings of the Philosophy of Education Society of Great Britain*, vol. 6, no. 1, January 1972, 37). For a clear example of a disguised but important programmatic definition of *school*, see Oakeshott's essay "Education: The Engagement and Its Frustration" in *Proceedings of the Philosophy of Education Society of Great Britain*, vol. 5, no. 1, January 1971, 43-76.

4 Peters, "Aims of Education: A Conceptual Inquiry" in *The Philosophy of Education*, 13. This point should not be interpreted as an attempt to underestimate the important work of R.S. Peters on the concepts of *aim* and *education.*

5 Hirst, *Knowledge and the Curriculum*, 3 (italics added).

6 Ibid., 3 and 7.

7 Ibid., 4.

8 "The Contribution of Philosophy to the Study of the Curriculum" in *Changing the Curriculum*, Kerr (ed.), 43.

9 Hirst, op. cit., 4 (italics added).

10 It is ironic that Hirst explicitly rejects this view of the mind in his book *Knowledge and the Curriculum.*

11 For a clear and useful discussion of these issues see Barrow, *Understanding Skills.*

12 For Hirst's thesis on the forms of knowledge, see his *Knowledge and the Curriculum.*

13 *Conditions of Knowledge*, 2 (italics added).

CHAPTER FOUR

1 L. Wittgenstein, *Zettel*, #419.

2 The first modern writer to talk about such a paradox is Peters in his essay "Habit and Reason: The Paradox of Moral Education," reprinted in Peters, *Psychology and Ethical Development*. For subsequent discussions of the paradox, see: Kazepides, "What Is the Paradox of Moral Education?" and "The Alleged Paradox of Moral Education" in *The Domain of Moral Education*, Cochran et al. (eds). Also: Gardner, "On Some Paradoxes of Moral Education," *Journal of Philosophy of Education,* and "The Paradox of Moral Education: A Reassessment," ibid.

3 See my discussion of the views of Durkheim and Hudson in "Educating, Socializing and Indoctrinating," in *Journal of Philosophy of Education* 16, 2.

4 Peters, op. cit., 272

5 Peters, op. cit., 268

6 It is not made clear by Peters how what he called the paradox of moral education can be resolved by an analysis of the concept of habit given his statement of the paradox: "given that it is desirable to develop people who conduct themselves rationally, intelligently and with a fair degree of spontaneity, *the brute facts* of child development reveal that at the most formative years of a child's development he is incapable of this form of life and impervious to the proper way of passing it on," op. cit., 271 (italics added).

7 Peters states: "All sorts of things are picked up in this way – desirable things such as a passion for poetry, nuances of style and argument, objectivity towards facts, respect for persons; undesirable things such as partisan allegiances, contempt for people of different persuasions, bad manners, and class-consciousness; and trivial things such as mannerisms, a tone of voice, gestures," in *The Concept of Education*, Peters (ed.), 11.

8 Hume, *A Treatise of Human Nature*, 92.

9 Gill, "On Reaching Bedrock," *Metaphilosophy*, vol. 5, no. 4, 280.

10 Kant, *Critique of Pure Reason*, 56, as quoted in Gill above.

11 Wittgenstein, *On Certainty*, #204 (Hereafter: O.C.).

12 Wittgenstein, *P.I.*, #485.

13 Ibid., #481.

14 Wittgenstein, ibid., #110.

15 *Nachlass,* as quoted by Hallett in *A Companion...*, #110, 235.
16 Ibid., #229, 1316.
17 Wittgenstein, *O.C.*, #225.
18 Wittgenstein, *Zettel*, #545 (Hereafter: *Z*).
19 Kazepides, "Wittgenstein and the Rationalists on Learning and Teaching," *Philosophy of Education*, Proceedings of the Philosophy of Education Society, 328.
20 Wittgenstein, *O.C.*, #152.
21 Ibid., #211.
22 Ibid., #341.
23 Ibid., #403.
24 Ibid., #657.
25 Ibid., #210.
26 Ibid., #94.
27 Wittgenstein, *P.I.*, II, 226.
28 Wittgenstein, *O.C.*, #359.
29 Ibid, #425.
30 Ibid., #287.
31 Wittgenstein, *P.I.*, #472.
32 Ibid., #473.
33 Ibid., #474.
34 Wittgenstein, *Lectures and Conversations*, 56.
35 Wittgenstein, *Z.*, #540-1.
36 Wittgenstein, *O.C.*, #402.
37 Wittgenstein, *Z.*, #545.
38 Ibid., #101.
39 Ibid., #391.
40 Phillips, *Wittgenstein and Scientific Knowledge,* 34.
41 Wittgenstein, *O.C.*, #105 (italics added).
42 Phillips, op. cit., 35.
43 Wittgenstein, *O.C.*, #94.
44 Ibid., #94, 99.
45 Ibid., #468, 281, 155, 662, 25.
46 Ibid., #312, 56, 360.
47 Kazepides, "Indoctrination, Doctrines and the Foundations of Rationality."
48 Wittgenstein, *O.C.*, 53.
49 Ibid., #108.

50 Wittgenstein, *Z.*, #339.
51 Wittgenstein, *O.C.*, #279.
52 Ibid., #160.
53 Ibid., #208.
54 Kazepides, "Wittgenstein and the Rationalists on Learning and Teaching." *Philosophy of Education*, Proceedings of the Philosophy of Education Society, 1986, 323-34.
55 Wittgenstein, *O.C.*, #559.
56 *The Philosophical Review*, vol. 74, no. 1, January 1965.
57 Wittgenstein, *O.C.*, #155.
58 Ibid., #156.
59 Ibid., #160.
60 Ibid., #152.
61 Aristotle, *Nichomachean Ethics*, book II, 3, 4 (italics added).
62 Wittgenstein, O.C., 208.
63 Wilson, "Moral Components and Moral Education," 181.
64 Ibid. (the last four italics have been added).
65 Wittgenstein, *P.I.*, #199, 180.

CHAPTER FIVE

1 Plato, *Sophist*, 263e.
2 Plato, *Theaetetus*, 190.
3 Nahm, *Early Greek Philosophy*, 203.
4 Goethe, *Faust*, quoted in Wittgenstein in *On Certainty*, #402.
5 Oakeshott, *The Voice of Liberal Learning*, 42.
6 Ibid., 63.
7 Ibid., 133.
8 The word *logos* in ancient Greek has over forty uses, all of which have something to do with human reason. Here are some of them: explanation, ground, argument, rule, principle, debate, narrative, common talk, maxim, sentence.
9 Bohm and Peat, *Science, Order and Creativity*, 241.
10 Habermas, *Communication and the Evolution of Society*, 3.
11 Freire, *Pedagogy of the Oppressed* and *Pedagogy of Hope*.
12 Gadamer, *Truth and Method*, 347, 143.
13 Wittgenstein, *O.C.*, #252, 211, 341.
14 Aristotle, *Nichomachean Ethics*, I, vii, 13-16.

15 Democritus, #53.
16 Oakeshott, op. cit., 60-2.
17 Ibid., 98.
18 Heraclitus, #94.

CHAPTER SIX

1 See Dawson and Prewitt, *Political Socialization*, 7, and Stewart and Glynn, *Introduction to Sociology*, 74.
2 Cooley, *Social Organization*, 23-31.
3 Ibid., 30.
4 Mead, *Mind, Self and Society*, 135.
5 Durkheim, *Education and Sociology*, 71.
6 Ibid.
7 Dewey, *Democracy and Education*, 50.
8 Durkheim, op. cit., 64.
9 Ibid.
10 Williams, *Morality: An Introduction*, 21.
11 Ibid.
12 Even the notorious Trofim Lysenko, who tried to revive Lamarckian views of heredity in the Soviet Union with the help of Stalin and the Central Committee of the Communist Party, was not promoting a doctrine but a defunct theory that happened to agree with the prevailing political ideology in that country. His views were not, in principle, unfalsifiable, and they have been abandoned because they were part of political propaganda.
13 Strawson, *Individuals*, xiii.
14 Austin, *Philosophical Papers*, 130-3.
15 Snook, *Indoctrination and Education*, 32.
16 White makes that claim in "Indoctrination," in *The Concept of Education*, Peters (ed.), 183.
17 For a discussion of the alleged doctrines contained in Darwin's theory see Sober, *The Nature of Selection*, chapter 2.
18 McClellan, *Philosophy of Education*, 142-3.
19 Wittgenstein, *C. and V.*, 29e.
20 Wittgenstein, *Lectures and Conversations*, 56.
21 Wittgenstein, op. cit., 50e.
22 Ibid., 64e.

23 Wittgenstein, op. cit., 58.
24 Ibid., 59.
25 Snook, *Indoctrination and Education*, 35.
26 Green, "Indoctrination and Beliefs," in Snook (ed.), *Concepts of Indoctrination*, 44-5.
27 Morawetz, *Wittgenstein and Knowledge*, 75.
28 Wittgenstein, O.C., #538.
29 Ibid., #243.
30 Wittgenstein, *C. and V.*, 28e.
31 Hawkings, *A Brief History of Time*.

CHAPTER SEVEN

1 It was Hirst who in his *Knowledge and the Curriculum* first introduced the idea of the forms of knowledge and the criteria that enable us to distinguish them as such; the present discussion differs from his in some significant respects.
2 Wittgenstein, *C. and V.*, 30e.
3 *Corinthians*, chapter 13, 13.
4 Mallach, *Fragmenta Philosophorum*, iii, 7.
5 Quoted by Harpur in *The Pagan Christ*, 115.
6 Plato, *Phaedo*, 89b.
7 *Mathew*, 5.
8 Ibid., 13, 49-50.
9 One of the truly primitive Byzantine hymns of the Greek Church says: "God is with us. Know ye (other) nations, you will be defeated, for God is with us."
10 Plato, *Phaedo*, 89, d.
11 For clear and forceful counterarguments to the existence of God, see, among many others, Simon Blackburn, *Think*, 1999.

CHAPTER EIGHT

1 Kathleen Freeman, *Ancilla to the Presocratic Philosophers*, 27.
2 Some relevant views can be found in the following works: Kroeber, *Anthropology Today*;. Kluchohn, *Culture and Behavior*; White, *The Science of Culture*; Kroeber and Kluchohn, *Culture*; Supir, *Culture, Language and Personality*.

3 Plato, *Republic*, 3, 414e.
4 Ibid., 3, 415e.
5 *Romans*, 7, 21-5.
6 Pagels, *Adam, Eve and the Serpent*, chapters 5 and 6.
7 Ibid., 145.
8 Rousseau, *Emile*, 56.
9 Maslow, *Toward a Psychology of Being*, 4. See also *The Farther Reaches of Human Nature*.
10 Rousseau, Ibid.
11 Sartre, *Existentialism and Human Emotions*.
12 Ibid., 16.
13 Oakeshott, "Education: The Engagement and Its Frustration," in *Education and the Development of Reason*, Dearden (ed.), 20.
14 Ibid., 19-21.
15 Ibid., 21-2.
16 Peters, "The Justification of Education," in *The Philosophy of Education*, 253.
17 Ibid., 254-5.
18 Democritus B33 (Herman Diets's numbering).

Bibliography

Adkins, A.W.H., *From the Many to the One*, London: Constable, 1970.

Aeschylus, *Prometheus Bound*.

Alston, William, *Philosophy of Language*, Englewood Cliffs, New Jersey: Prentice Hall, 1964.

– *Perceiving God: The Epistemology of Religious Experience*, Cornell University Press, 1991.

Aristotle, *The Nichomachean Ethics*.

Audi, Robert, *The Architecture of Reason*, Oxford University Press, 2001.

Austin, J.L., *Philosophical Papers*, Oxford: Clarendon Press, 1961.

– *How to Do Things with Words*, New York: Oxford University Press, 1965.

Barrow, Robin, *Understanding Skills*, London, ON: The Althouse Press, 1990.

Benhabib, Seyla, *The Claims of Culture*, Princeton: Princeton University Press, 2002.

The Bible.

Black, Max, *Models and Metaphors*, Ithaca, NY: Cornell University Press, 1962.

Blackburn, Simon, *Think*, Oxford University Press, 1999.

– *Plato's Republic: A Biography*, Vancouver/Toronto: Douglas & McIntyre, 2007.

Bohm, David, *Unfolding Meaning: A Weekend of Dialogue with David Bohm*, London: Routledge, 1987.

– and Peat, D., *Science, Order and Creativity*, New York: Bantam, 1987.

Bonnefoy, Yves, *Greek and Egyptian Mythologies*, Chicago: University of Chicago Press, 1992.

Budd, Malcolm, *Wittgenstein's Philosophy of Psychology*, London: Routledge, 1989.

Bury, J.B., *History of the Late Roman Empire*, New York: Dover Publications, 1958.

Carpendale, Jeremy I., and Lewis, Charlie, "Constructing an Understanding of Mind: The Development of Children's Social Understanding within Social Interaction," *Behavioral and Brain Sciences*, 27, 79-151, 2004.

Carr, David, *Educating the Virtues*, London: Routledge, 1991.

– "Rival Conceptions of Practice in Education and Teaching," *Journal of Philosophy of Education*, 37, 2, May 2003.

Cavell, Stanley, *Must We Mean What We Say?* New York: Charles Scribner's and Sons, 1969.

Chomsky, Noam, *Language and Responsibility*, New York: Pantheon Books, 1977.

– *Understanding Power*, New York: The New Press, 2002.

Cooley, Charles H., Social Organization, New York: Free Press, 1958.

Dawkins, Richard, *The God Delusion*, New York: Houghton Mifflin Company, 2006.

Dawson, R.E., and Prewitt, K., *Political Socialization*, Boston, Little, Brown & Co, 1969.

Dearden, R.F., Hirst, P.H., and Peters, R.S., *Education and the Development of Reason*, London: Routledge and Kegan Paul, 1972.

Democritus, *B33* (Herman Diets's numbering).

Dewey, John, *Democracy and Education*, New York: The Macmillan Company, 1961.

Dostal, Robert J., *The Cambridge Companion to Gadamer*, Cambridge University Press, 2002.

Durkheim, Emile, *Education and Sociology*, New York: The Free Press, 1956.

Egan, Kieran, *The Educated Mind*, The University of Chicago Press, 1991.

Foot, Philipa, *Virtues and Vices*, Berkeley: University of California Press, 1978.

Freeman, Kathleen, *Ancilla to the Presocratic Philosophers*, Cambridge, MA: Harvard University Press, 1978.

Freire, Paulo, *Pedagogy of the Oppressed*, New York: The Seabury Press, 1973.

– *Pedagogy of Hope: Reviving Pedagogy of the Oppressed*, New York: Continuum Publishing Company, 1994.

Fromm, Eric, and Xirau, Ramon (eds), *The Nature of Man*, New York, NY: The Macmillan Company, 1971.

Gadamer, Hans-Georg, *Truth and Method*, London: Sheed and Ward, 1979.

– *Philosophical Hermeneutics* (Translated and edited by David E. Linge), Berkeley: University of California Press, 1997.

Gardner, Martin, *Fads and Fallacies*, New York: Dover publications, 1957.

Gardner, P., "On Some Paradoxes of Moral Education," *Journal of Philosophy of Education* 15, 1, 1981.

– "The Paradox of Moral Education: A Reassessment," *Journal of Philosophy of Education* 19, 1, 1985.

Garver, Newton, *This Complicated Form of Life: Essays on Wittgenstein*, Chicago: Open Court, 1994.

Gert, Bernard, *Morality: A New Justification of the Moral Rules*, Oxford University Press, 1988.

Gill, J.H., "On Reaching Bedrock," *Metaphilosophy*, vol. 5, no. 4, 280, 1974.

Gonzales, Francisco J., *Dialectic and Dialogue: Plato's Practice of Philosophical Inquiry*, Evanston, IL: Northwestern University Press, 1998.

Graves, Robert, *The Greek Myths* (vols 1-2), London: The Folio Society, 1996.

Habermas, Jurgen, *Legitimation Crisis*, London: Heinemann, 1973.

– *Communication and the Evolution of Society*, London: Heinemann, 1979.

– *The Theory of Communicative Action* (Volume 1), Cambridge: Polity Press, 1984.

Haller, Rudolf, *Questions on Wittgenstein*, Lincoln: University of Nebraska Press, 1988.

Hallett, Garth, *A Companion to Wittgenstein's "Philosophical Investigations,"* Ithaca: NY: Cornell University Press, 1977.

Hamilton, Edith, *Mythology*, Boston: Little, Brown and Company, 1942.

Hare, William, *Open-Mindedness and Education*, Montreal: McGill-Queen's University Press, 1979.

Harpur, Thomas, *The Pagan Christ*. New York: Walker and Company, 2004.

Hawkings, S.W., *A Brief History of Time*. Toronto: Bantam Books, 1988.

Heidegger, Martin, *An Introduction to Metaphysics*, New York: Anchor Books, 1961.

– *Being and Time*, State University of New York Press, 1996.

Heraclitus, *Fragments* 40, 50, 119.

Hick, John, *Philosophy of Religion*, Englewood Cliffs, New Jersey: Prentice Hall, 1963.

Hirst, Paul H., *Knowledge and the Curriculum*, London: Routledge and Kegan Paul, 1974.

– and Peters, R.S., *The Logic of Education*, London: Routledge, 1970.

Howard, V.A., and Scheffler, Israel, *Work, Education and Leadership*, New York: Peter Lang, 1995.

Hume, D., *A Treatise of Human Nature* (ed. by L.A. Selby-Bigge), Oxford University Press, 1967.

Hursthouse, Rosalind, *On Virtue Ethics*, Oxford University Press, 1999.

Itard, Jean-Marc-Gaspard, *The Wild Boy of Aveyron,* New York, NY: Meredith Publishing Company, 1962,

Jaeger, Werner, *Paideia: The Ideals of Greek Culture*, vol. 1, New York: Oxford University Press, 1974.

Johnston, Paul, *Wittgenstein and Moral Philosophy*, New York: Routledge, 1989.

Kant, E., *Critique of Pure Reason* (translated by Norman Kemp-Smith), New York: St Martin's, 1965.

Kazepides, Tasos, "What Is the Paradox of Moral Education?" *Philosophy of Education 1969: Proceedings of the Philosophy of Education Society*. 1969.

– "On the Nature of Philosophical Questions and the Function of Philosophy in Education," *Philosophy of Education*, Philosophy of Education Society, 1970.

– "On Learning from the Consequences of One's Actions," *Oxford Review of Education*. vol. 4, no. 1, 1978, 77-84.
– "The Alleged Paradox of Moral Education" *The Domain of Moral Education*, D.B. Cochrane, C.M. Hamm, and A.C. Kazepides (eds), New York: Paulist Press, 1979.
– "Human Nature in Its Educational Dimensions" *Journal of Philosophy of Education*, vol. 13, 1979.
– "Educating, Socializing and Indoctrinating," *Journal of Philosophy of Education*, 16, 2, 1982.
– "Wittgenstein and the Rationalists on Learning and Teaching," *Philosophy of Education 1986*, Normal, IL: Philosophy of Education Society, 1986.
– "Indoctrination, Doctrines and the Foundations of Rationality," *Philosophy of Education 1987: Proceedings of the Philosophy of Education Society*, Normal, IL: Philosophy of Education Society, 1987.
– "On Educational Aims, Curriculum Objectives and the Preparation of Teachers," *Journal of Philosophy of Education*, vol. 23, no. 1, 1989, 51-9.
– "On the Prerequisites of Moral Education: A Wittgensteinean Perspective," *Journal of Philosophy of Education*, vol. 25, no. 2, 1991.
– "'Assembling Reminders for a Particular Purpose': The Nature and Function of Educational Theory," *Canadian Journal of Education*, vol. 19, 4, 1994.
– *The Philosophy of Education* (in Greek, second edition), Thessaloniki: Vanias Publications, 1998.
– *Dialogue: Its Importance and Its Enemies* (in Greek) Thessaloniki: Vanias Publications, 2004.
Kluchohn, Clyde, *Culture and Behavior*, New York: Free Press of Glencoe, 1962.
Kroeber, A.L. (ed.), *Anthropology Today*, University of Chicago Press, 1953.
Kroeber, A.L., and Kluchohn, Clyde, *Culture: Critical Review of Concepts and Definitions*. New York: Vintage Books, 1952.
Lakoff, George, and Turner, Mark, *More than Cool Reason: A Field Guide to Poetic Metaphor*, Chicago: The University of Chicago Press, 1989.

Lipman, M., *Thinking in Education*, New York: Cambridge University Press, 1991.

Livingston, John A., *Rogue Primate: An Exploration of Human Domestication*, Toronto: Key Porter Books Ltd, 1994.

Lorrington, Carolyne (ed.), *The Woman's Companion to Mythology*, London: HarperCollins, 1992.

MacIntyre, Alasdair, *After Virtue: A Study in Moral Theory*, Notre Dame, IN: University of Notre Dame Press, 1981.

– *Dependent Rational Animal*, Chicago: Open Court, 1999.

Mackie, J.L., Ethics: *Inventing Right and Wrong*, London: Penguin Books, 1990.

Malcolm, Norman, *Ludwig Wittgenstein: A Memoir*, Oxford University Press, 1958.

Maslow, Abraham H., *Toward a Psychology of Being*, Toronto: D. Van Nostrand Co., 1968.

– *The Farther Reaches of Human Nature*, Toronto: Penguin, 1971.

Mason, Richard, *Understanding Understanding*, Albany, NY: State University of New York Press, 2003.

McCarthy, Thomas, *The Critical Theory of Jurgen Habermas*, Cambridge, MA: The MIT Press, 1979.

McClellan, James E., *Philosophy of Education*, Englewood Cliffs, NJ: Prentice-Hall, Inc., 1976.

McPeck, John E., *Critical Thinking and Education*, Oxford: Martin Robertson, 1981.

Mead, George Herbert, *Mind, Self and Society*, University of Chicago Press, 1934.

Morawetz, Thomas, *Wittgenstein and Knowledge: The Importance of On Certainty*, New York: Humanities Press, 1980.

Murdoch, Iris, *The Fire and the Sun: Why Plato Banished the Artists*, Oxford University Press, 1977.

– *Metaphysics as a Guide to Morals*, London: Penguin Books, 1992.

Nagel, Thomas, *The Possibility of Altruism*, New Jersey: Princeton University Press, 1970.

– *The Last Word*, New York: Oxford University Press, 1997.

Nahm, M.C., *Early Greek Philosophy*, New York: Appleton-Century-Crofts, 1964.

Oakeshott, Michael, *Rationalism in Politics and Other Essays*, London: Methuen, 1962.

– *The Voice of Liberal Learning* (ed. by Timothy Fuller), New Haven: Yale University Press, 1989.

Pagels, Elaine, *Adam, Eve and the Serpent*, New York: Random House, 1988.

– *The Gnostic Gospels*, New York: Random House, 1979.

Passmore, John, *The Philosophy of Teaching*, Harvard University Press, 1980.

Peters, R. S., "Habit and Reason: The Paradox of Moral Education" *Moral Education in a Changing Society*, W.R. Niblett (ed.), London: Faber, 1963.

– *Ethics and Education*, London: George Allen and Unwin, Ltd, 1966.

– "What Is an Educational Process?" *The Concept of Education*, London: Routledge and Kegan Paul, 1967.

– "Aims of Education – A Conceptual Inquiry," *The Philosophy of Education*, Oxford University Press, 1973.

– *Authority, Responsibility and Education*, London: George Allen and Unwin Ltd, 1973.

– *Reason and Compassion*, London: Routledge and Kegan Paul, 1973.

– *Psychology and Ethical Development*, London: Allen and Unwin, 1974.

– *Education and the Education of Teachers*, London: Routledge and Kegan Paul, 1977.

Phillips, D.L., *Wittgenstein and Scientific Knowledge*, London: Macmillan Press, 1977.

Pincoffs, Edmund L., *Quandaries and Virtues: Against Reductivism in Ethics*, University Press of Kansas, 1986.

Plato, *The Collected Dialogues*, New York: Pantheon Books, 1961.

– *Apology.*

– *Euthyphro.*

– *Theaetetus.*

– Sophist.

– *Phaedo.*

– *Republic.*

Popper, Karl, *The Open Society and Its Enemies* (vols 1-2), New York: Harper and Row Publishers, 1962.

Rachels, James, *The Elements of Moral Philosophy*, McGraw-Hill Inc., 1993.

Ricoeur, Paul, *The Rule of Metaphor: Multidisciplinary Studies of the Creation of Meaning*, Toronto: University of Toronto Press, 1977.

Robinson, John Mason, *An Introduction to Early Greek Philosophy*, Boston: Houghton Mifflin Company, 1968.

Rousseau, Jean Jacques, *Emile* (trans. B. Foxley), New York: Everyman's Library, 1911.

Russell, Bertrand, *Why I Am Not a Christian*, New York: Simon & Schuster, 1957.

Ryle, Gilbert, *The Concept of Mind*, New York: Barnes and Noble, 1949.

– "Philosophical Arguments," *Logical Positivism*, A.J. Ayer (ed.), New York: The Free Press, 1959.

– "The Theory of Meaning," *Philosophy and Ordinary Language*, Charles E. Caton, (ed.), Urbana: University of Illinois Press, 1963.

– "Ordinary Language" *Ordinary Language*, V.C. Chappell (ed.), New Jersey, Englewood Cliffs: Prentice Hall, 1964.

Sartre, Jean-Paul, *Existentialism and Human Emotions*, New York: Philosophical Library, 1957.

Scheffler, Israel, *The Language of Education*, Springfield, IL: Charles C. Thomas Publisher, 1960.

– *Conditions of Knowledge*, The University of Chicago Press, 1965.

– *Science and Subjectivity*, New York: The Bobbs-Merrill Company, 1967.

– *Reason and Teaching*, New York: The Bobbs-Merrill Company, 1973.

– *Of Human Potential*, London: Routledge and Kegan Paul, 1985.

Schulte, Joachim, *Wittgenstein: An Introduction*, State University of New York Press, 1992.

Searle, John R., *Minds, Brains and Science*, Harvard University Press, 1984.

– *The Construction of Social Reality*, New York: The Free Press, 1995.

Siegel, Harvey, *Educating Reason*, New York: Routledge, 1988.

Singer, Peter, *The Expanding Circle: Ethics and Sociobiology*, New York: New American Library, 1981.

Snell, Bruno, *The Discovery of the Mind: The Greek Origins of European Thought*, New York: Harper and Brothers, 1960.

Snook, I.A., *Indoctrination and Education*, London: Routledge and Kegan Paul, 1972.

– (ed.), *Concepts of Indoctrination*, London: Routledge and Kegan Paul, 1972.

Sober, Elliott, *The Nature of Selection: Evolutionary Theory in Philosophical Focus*, Cambridge, MA: The MIT Press, 1984.

Soltis, Jonas F., *An Introduction to the Analysis of Educational Concepts*, Reading, MA: Addison-Wesley Publishing Company, 1978.

Sophocles, *Antigone.*

Stewart, E.W., and Glynn, L.A., *Introduction to Sociology,* New York: McGraw-Hill, 1979.

Strawson, P.F., "Construction and Analysis" *The Revolution in Philosophy*, Ayer et al. (eds), New York: St Martin's Press, 1956.

– *Individuals*, New York: Doubleday and Co., Inc., l963.

Strike, Kenneth A., and Soltis, Jonas, F. *The Ethics of Teaching*, New York: Teachers College Press, 1985.

Supir, Edward, *Culture, Language and Personality*, Berkeley: University of California Press, 1966.

Swanton, Christine, *Virtue Ethics: A Pluralistic View*, Oxford University Press, 2003.

Taylor, Charles, *Sources of the Self*, Cambridge, MA: Harvard University Press, 1989.

– *Modern Social Imaginaries*, Durham: Duke University Press, 2004.

Taylor, Richard, *Human Agency and Language*, Cambridge: Cambridge University Press, 1985.

Toulmin, Stephen, *Knowing and Acting: An Invitation to Philosophy*, New York: Macmillan Publishing Co., Inc., 1976.

Vygotsky, Lev Semenovich, *Thought and Language*. Cambridge, MA: The MIT Press, 1962

– *Mind in Society*, Harvard University Press, 1978.

Waismann, F., *The Principles of Linguistic Philosophy*, edited by R. Harre, New York: St Martin's Press, 1965.

Walzer, Michael, *Thick and Thin: Moral Argument at Home and Abroad*, Notre Dame: University of Notre Dame Press, 1994.

Weinberg, Julius R., and Yandell, Keity E., *Philosophy of Religion*, New York: Holt, Rinehart and Winston, Inc., 1971.

West, M.L., *Hesiod, Works and Days*, Oxford: Clarendon Press, 1978.

– *Hesiod, Theogony*, Oxford: Clarendon Press, 1996.

White, John, *The Aims of Education Restated*, London: Routledge & Kegan Paul, 1982.

White, Leslie A., *The Science of Culture*, New York: Grove Press Inc., 1949.

Whitehead, Alfred North, *The Aims of Education*, New York: Mentor Books, 1958.

Williams, Bernard, *Morality: An Introduction,* New York: Harper & Row, 1972.

– *Moral Luck*, Cambridge: Cambridge University Press, 1981.

Wilson, Edward O., *On Human Nature*, Harvard University Press, 1978.

Wilson, John, "Moral Components and Moral Education: A Reply to Francis Dunlop," *The Domain of Moral Education*, D.B Cochrane, C.M. Hamm, and A.C. Kazepides (eds), New York: Paulist Press, 1979.

Wittgenstein, Ludwig, *Philosophical Investigations* (translated by G.E.M. Anscombe), New York: The Macmillan Company, 1953.

– *Tractatus Logicophilosophicus*, New York: Humanities Press, 1961.

– *Lectures and Conversations on Aesthetics, Psychology and Religious Belief*, Berkley: University of California Press, 1967.

– *On Certainty* (translated by D. Paul and G.E.M. Anscombe), New York: Harper and Row Publishers, 1969.

– *Philosophische Bemergungen* (edited by R. Rhees), Frankfurt on the Main, 1969.

– *Zettel* (translated by G.E.M. Uncombed), Berkeley: University of California Press, 1970.

– *Culture and Value*, Oxford: Basil Blackwell, 1977.

Index